I0491094

ARTBOOKS

FROM CRESCENT MOON
PUBLISHING

Leonardo da Vinci
by James Pearson

Early Netherlandish Painting
by Rosalind Mutter

Memling
By W.H.J. & J.C. Weale

Van Eyck
By J. Cyril M. Weale

Piero della Francesca
by Naomi Haskell

Giovanni Bellini
by Julia Davis

Eric Gill: Nuptials of God
by Anthony Hoyland

*Minimal Art and Artists In the
1960s and After*
by Laura Garrard

*Vincent van Gogh: Visionary
Landscapes*
by Stuart Morris

*Mark Rothko: The Art of
Transcendence*
by Julia Davis

Jasper Johns
by L.M. Poole

Brice Marden
by Laura Garrard

*Frank Stella: American Abstract
Artist*
by James Pearson

*Maurice Sendak and the Art of
Children's Book Illustration*
by L.M. Poole

*Sex in Art: Pornography and
Pleasure in Painting and
Sculpture*
by Cassidy Hughes

The Art of Andy Goldsworthy
by William Malpas

*Andy Goldsworthy: Touching
Nature*
by William Malpas

Andy Goldsworthy In Close-Up
by William Malpas

Andy Goldsworthy In America
by William Malpas

Andy Goldsworthy: Pocket Guide
by William Malpas

The Art of Richard Long
by William Malpas

Richard Long: Pocket Guide
by William Malpas

*Constantin Brancusi: Sculpting the
Essence of Things*
by James Pearson

*Alison Wilding: The Embrace of
Sculpture*
by Susan Quinnell

Erotic Art In the 19th Century
By Cassidy Hughes

Erotic Art In the Renaissance
By Cassidy Hughes

Erotic Art
By Cassidy Hughes

Whistler
By T. Martin Wood

Rodin: The Man and His Art
Edited by Judith Cladel

Rodin
By Rainer Maria Rilke

Auguste Rodin
By Camille Mauclair

Corot
By Sidney Allnutt

Fra Angelico
By Jennie Ellis Keysor

Fra Angelico
By James Mason

Fra Angelico
By J.B. Supino

Aubrey Beardsley
By Robert Ross

The Art of Aubrey Beardsley
By Arthur Symons

Leighton
By Ernest Rhys

Millais
By A. Lys Baldry

The Madonna In Art
By Estelle Hurll

Women In the Fine Arts
By Clara Erskine Clement

The Venetian School of Painting
By Evelyn Phillipps

Boucher
By Haldane McFall

Fragonard
By Haldane McFall

Leonardo da Vinci
By Maurice Brockwell

Famous European Painters
By Sarah Bolton

Great Artists
By Jennie Ellis Keysor

Great Pictures
Edited by Esther Singleton

Knights of Art
By Amy Steedman

Delacroix
By Paul Konody

Ingres
By A.J. Finberg

Goya
By Francis Crastre

Dürer
By Hertbert Furst

Albrecht Dürer
By T. Sturge Moore

Dürer
By M.F. Sweetser

Rembrandt van Rijn
By Malcolm Bell

Rembrandt and His Works
By John Burnet

Rembrandt and His Etchings
By Louis Holman

Rembrandt
By Estelle M. Hurll

Rembrandt
By Josef Israels

Turner
By C. Lewis Hind

Turner
By W. Cosmo Monkhouse

The Art of Katsuhiro Otomo
By Jeremy Robinson

The Art of Masamune Shirow
By Jeremy Robinson

GIOTTO

GIOTTO

INTRODUCED BY JULIA CARTWRIGHT

CRESCENT MOON

First published 1902. This edition © 2021. Reprint 2023.

Set in Book Antiqua 10 on 14pt.
Designed by Radiance Graphics.

All rights reserved. No part of this book may be reprinted or reproduced, stored in a retrieval system, or transmitted, in any form or by any means, electronic, mechanical, photocopying, recording or otherwise, without permission from the publisher.

Images are used for information and research purposes, with no infringement of copyright or rights intended.

Thanks to the authors and publishers quoted.

British Library Cataloguing in Publication data

ISBN-13 9781861717221
ISBN-13 9781861718921

CRESCENT MOON PUBLISHING
P.O. Box 1312, Maidstone, Kent, ME14 5XU
Great Britain, www.crmoon.com

CONTENTS

NOTE ON THE TEXT

The text is from *Giotto*, in the *Masters In Art* series, introduced by Julia Cartwright, and published by Bates & Guild Company, Boston, 1902 (part 32, volume 3).

The illustrations in the original text are included in the illustrations section, along with many other works.

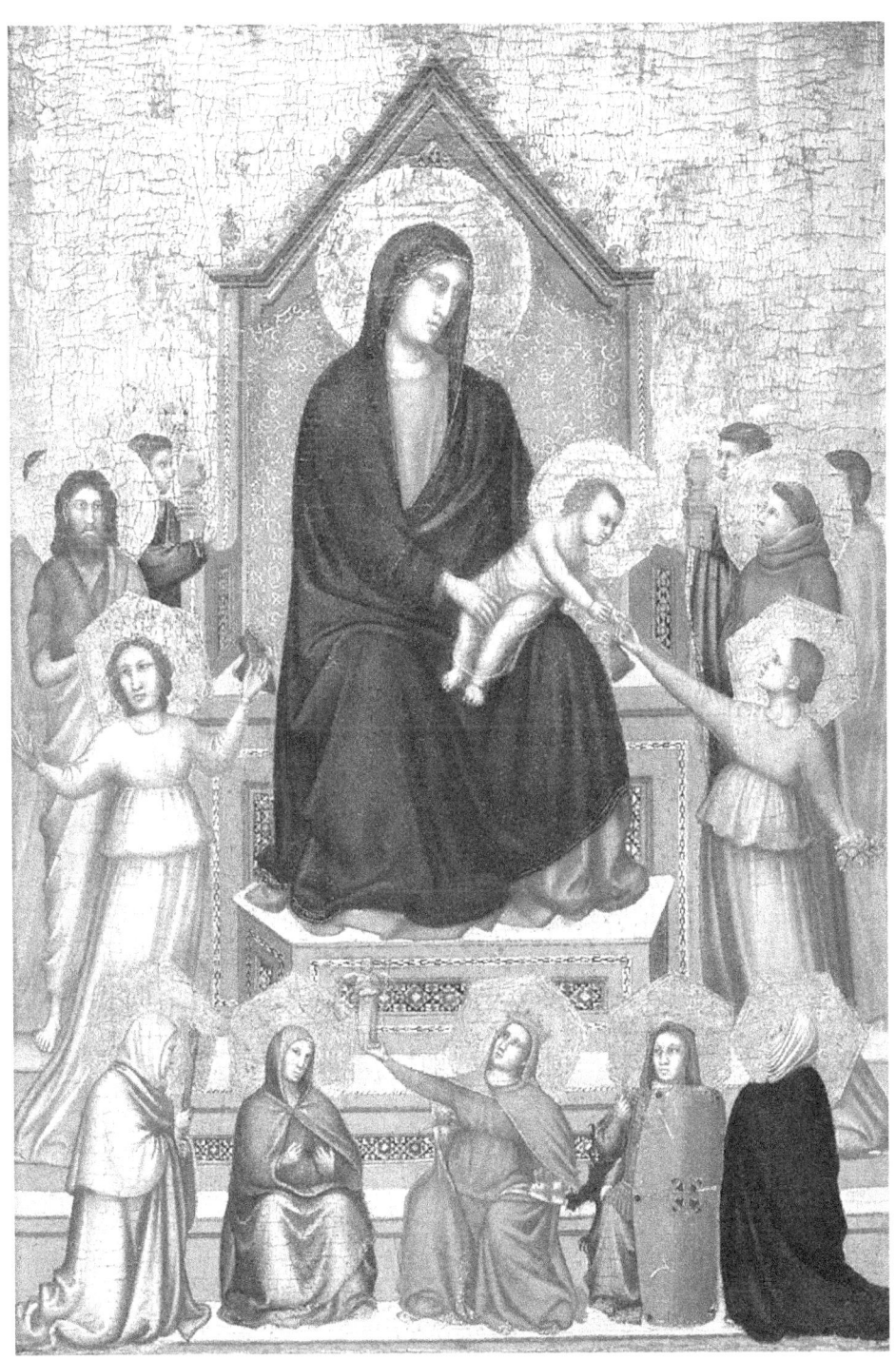

Giotto, Madonna Enthroned, 1315-20.

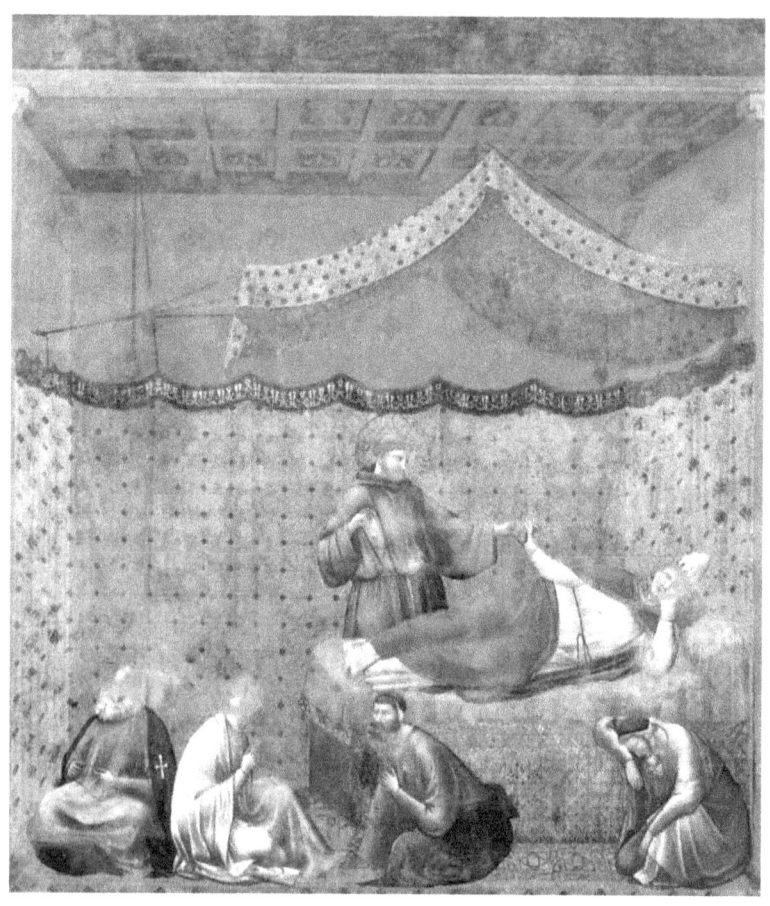

Giotto, The Dream of St Gregory, The Legend of St Francis

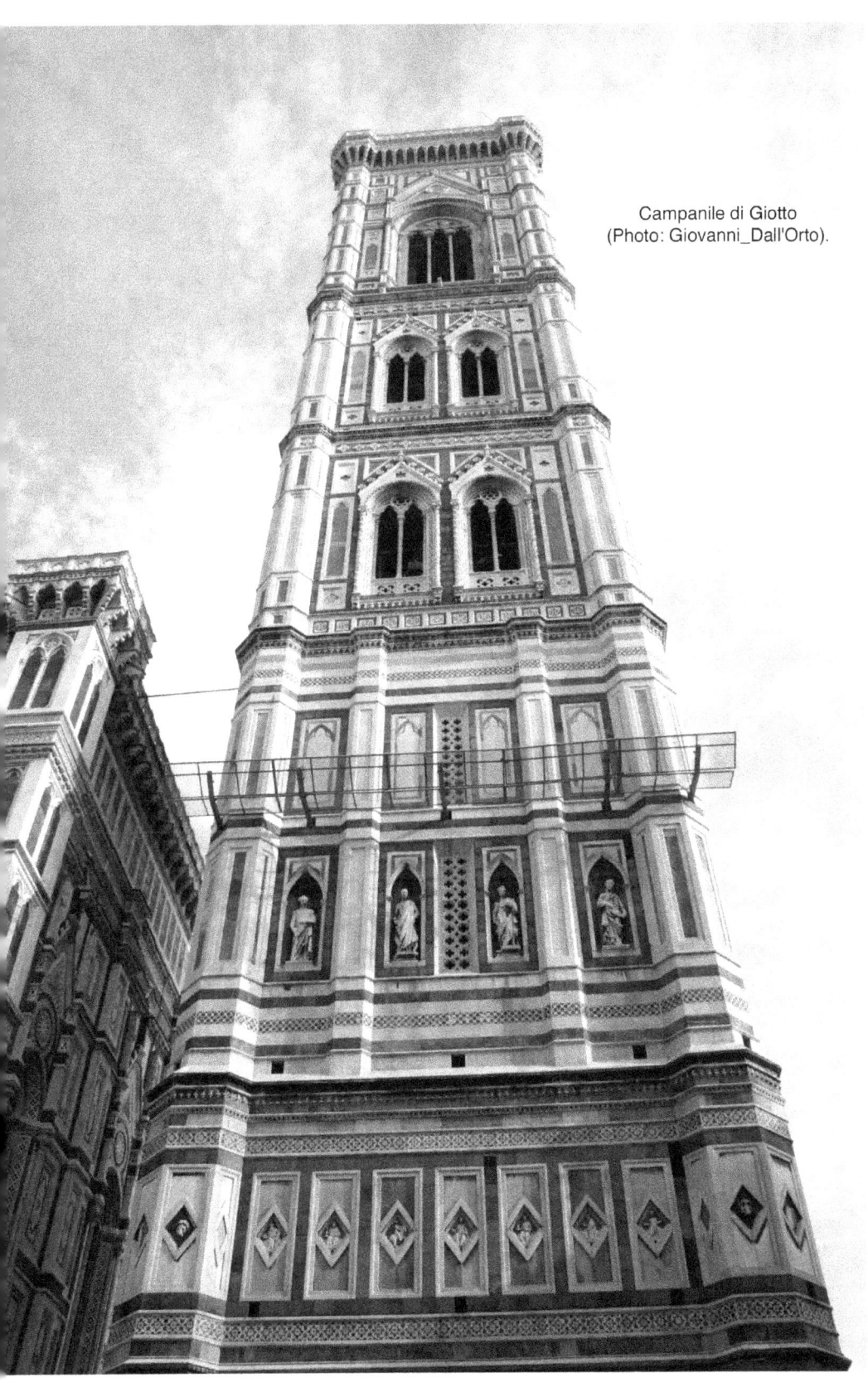

Campanile di Giotto
(Photo: Giovanni_Dall'Orto).

GIOTTO

BY JULIA CARTWRIGHT
– 'THE PAINTERS OF FLORENCE'

GIOTTO DI BONDONE
BORN 1266 (?): DIED 1337
FLORENTINE SCHOOL

"In a village of Etruria," writes Ghiberti, the oldest historian of the Florentine Renaissance, "Painting took her rise." In other words, Giotto di Bondone[1] was born, between 1265 and 1270, at Colle, in the Commune of Vespignano, a village of the Val Mugello fourteen miles from Florence. There the boy, who had been called Angiolo, after his grandfather, and went by the nickname of Angiolotto, or Giotto, kept his father's flocks on the grassy slopes of the Apennines, and was found one day by Cimabue, as he rode over the hills, drawing a sheep with a sharp stone upon a rock. Full of surprise at the child's talent for drawing, the great painter asked him if he would go back with him to Florence; to which both the boy and his father, a poor peasant named Bondone, gladly agreed. Thus, at ten years old, Giotto was taken straight from the sheepfolds and apprenticed to

---

1 Pronounced Jot´toe dee Bon-doe´nay.

the first painter in Florence. Such is the story told by Ghiberti and confirmed by Leonardo da Vinci, who, writing half a century before Vasari, remarks that Giotto took nature for his guide, and began by drawing the sheep and goats which he herded on the rocks.

Another version of the story of Giotto's boyhood is that he was apprenticed to a wool-merchant of Florence, but that instead of going to work he spent his time in watching the artists in Cimabue's shop; upon which his father applied to the master who consented to teach the boy painting. The natural vivacity and intelligence of the young student soon made him a favorite in Cimabue's workshop, while his extraordinary aptitude for drawing became every day more apparent. The legends of his marvelous skill, the stories of the fly that Cimabue vainly tried to brush off his picture, of the round O which he drew before the pope's envoy with one sweep of his pencil, are proofs of the wonder and admiration which Giotto's attempts to follow nature more closely excited among his contemporaries. This latter story is told by Vasari as follows:

> "The pope sent one of his courtiers to Tuscany to ascertain what kind of man Giotto might be, and what were his works; that pontiff then proposing to have certain paintings executed in the Church of St. Peter. The messenger spoke first with many artists in Siena; then, having received designs from them, he proceeded to Florence, and repaired one morning to the workshop where Giotto was occupied with his labors. He declared the purpose of the pope, and finally requested to have a drawing that he might send it to his holiness. Giotto, who was very courteous, took a sheet of paper and a pencil dipped in a red color, then, resting his elbow on his side to form a sort of compass, with one turn of the hand he drew a circle, so perfect and exact that it was a marvel to behold. This done, he turned smiling to the courtier, saying, 'Here is your drawing.' 'Am I to have nothing more than this?' inquired the latter, conceiving himself to be jested with. 'That is enough and to spare,' returned Giotto. 'Send it with the rest, and you will see if it will not be recognized.' The messenger, unable to obtain anything more, went away very ill-satisfied and fearing that he had been fooled. Nevertheless, having despatched the other drawings to the pope with the names of those who had done them he sent that of

Giotto also, relating the mode in which he had made his circle, without moving his arm and without compasses; from which the pope, and such of the courtiers as were well versed in the subject, perceived how far Giotto surpassed all the other painters of his time."

No doubt the boldness and originality of his genius soon led Giotto to abandon the purely conventional style of art then in use, and to seek after a more natural and lifelike form of expression. And early in his career he was probably influenced by the example of the sculptor Giovanni Pisano, who was actively engaged on his great works in Tuscany and Umbria at this time. The earliest examples of Giotto's style that remain to us are some small panels at Munich; but a larger and better-known work is the 'Madonna Enthroned,' in the Academy at Florence, which, although archaic in type, has a vigor and reality that are wholly wanting in Cimabue's Madonna in the same room. But it is to Assisi that we must turn for a fuller record of Giotto's training and development.

Here, in the old Umbrian city where St. Francis had lived and died, was the great double church which the alms of Christendom had raised above his burial-place. Unfortunately the records of the Franciscan convent are silent as to the painters of the frescos which cover its walls, and neither Cimabue nor Giotto is once mentioned. But Ghiberti, Vasari, and the later Franciscan historian, Rudolphus, all agree in saying that Giotto came to Assisi with his master Cimabue and there painted the lower course of frescos in the nave of the Upper Church....

In 1298 Giotto was invited to Rome by Cardinal Stefaneschi, the pope's nephew and a generous patron of art. At his bidding Giotto designed the famous mosaic of the 'Navicella,' or 'Ship of the Church,' which hangs in the vestibule of St. Peter's. Little trace of the original work now remains. More worthy of study is the altar-piece which he painted for the cardinal, and which is still preserved in the sacristy of St. Peter's.

Pope Boniface, we are told by Vasari, was deeply impressed by Giotto's merits, and loaded him with honors and rewards; but the frescos which he was employed to paint in the old basilica of St. Peter's perished long ago, and the only work of his now remaining in Rome besides the 'Navicella,' is the damaged fresco of Pope Boniface proclaiming the Jubilee, on a pillar of the Lateran Church. This last painting proves that Giotto was in Rome during the year 1300, when both his fellow-citizens Dante and the historian Giovanni Villani were present in the Eternal City. The poet was an intimate friend of the painter; and, after his return to Florence, Giotto introduced Dante's portrait in an altar-piece of 'Paradise' which he painted for the chapel of the Podestà Palace. But since this chapel was burned down in 1332, and not rebuilt until after Giotto's death, the fresco of Dante, which was discovered some years ago on the walls of the present building, must have been copied by one of his followers from the original painting.

It was probably during an interval of his journey back to Florence, or on some other visit to Assisi during the next few years, that Giotto painted his frescos in the Lower Church of St. Francis in that city. Chief among these are the four great allegories on the vaulted roof above the high altar, illustrating the meaning of the three monastic Virtues, Obedience, Chastity, and Poverty, whom, according to the legend, the saint met walking on the road to Siena in the form of three fair maidens, and whom he held up to his followers as the sum of evangelical perfection.

These allegories are not the only works which Giotto executed in the Lower Church of Assisi. Ghiberti's statement that he painted almost the whole of the Lower Church is confirmed by Rudolphus, who mentions the series of frescos of the childhood of Christ and the 'Crucifixion' in the right transept as being by his hand. In their present ruined condition it is not easy to distinguish between the work of the master and that of his assistants; but the whole series bears the stamp of Giotto's invention.

The next important works which he painted were the frescos in the Arena Chapel at Padua, built in 1303, by Enrico Scrovegno, who two years later invited Giotto to decorate the interior with frescos. When Dante visited Padua, in 1306, he found his friend Giotto living there with his wife, Madonna Ciutà, and his young family, and was honorably entertained by the painter in his own house. The poet often watched Giotto at work, with his children, who were "as ill-favored as himself," playing around, and wondered how it was that the creations of his brain were so much fairer than his own offspring. Giotto's small stature and insignificant appearance seem to have been constantly the subject of his friends' good-humored jests; and Petrarch and Boccaccio both speak of him as an instance of rare genius concealed under a plain and ungainly exterior. But this unattractive appearance was redeemed by a kindly and joyous nature, a keen sense of humor, and unfailing cheerfulness, which made him the gayest and most pleasant companion....

The fame which Giotto already enjoyed beyond the walls of Florence was greatly increased by his works in Padua, and before he left there he received and executed many commissions. From Padua, Vasari tells us, he went on to the neighboring city of Verona, where he painted the portrait of Dante's friend and protector, Can Grande della Scala, as well as other works in the Franciscan church, and then proceeded to Ferrara and Ravenna at the invitation of the Este and Polenta princes. All his works in the cities of North Italy, however, have perished, and it is to Florence that we must turn for the third and last remaining cycle of his frescos.

The great Franciscan church of Santa Croce had been erected in the last years of the thirteenth century, and the proudest Florentine families hastened to build chapels at their own expense as a mark of their devotion to the popular saint. Four of these chapels were decorated with frescos by Giotto's hand, but were all whitewashed in 1714, when Santa Croce underwent a thorough restoration. The frescos which he painted in the Guigni and Spinelli chapels have been entirely destroyed; but within the last fifty years the whitewash has been successfully removed from the walls of the Bardi and Peruzzi chapels, and the finest of Giotto's works that remain to us have been brought to light. Here his unrivaled powers as a great epic painter are revealed, and we realize his intimate knowledge of human nature and his profound sympathy with every form of life.

The exact date of these frescos remains uncertain, but they were probably painted soon after 1320. Recent research has as yet thrown little light upon the chronology of Giotto's life, and all we can discover is an occasional notice of the works which he executed, or of the property which he owned in Florence. Vasari's statement, that he succeeded to Cimabue's house and shop in the Via del Cocomero, Florence, is borne out by the will of the Florentine citizen Rinuccio, who, dying in 1312, describes "the excellent painter Giotto di Bondone" as a parishioner of Santa Maria Novella, and bequeathes a sum of "five pounds of small florins" to keep a lamp burning night and day before a crucifix painted by the said master in the Dominican church.

Of Giotto's eight children, the eldest, Francesco, became a painter, and when his father was absent from Florence managed the small property which Giotto had inherited at his old home of Vespignano. The painter's family lived chiefly at this country home, of which Giotto himself was very fond; and contemporary writers give us pleasant glimpses of the great master's excursions to Val Mugello. Boccaccio tells us how one day, as Giotto and the learned advocate Messer Forese, who, like himself, was short and insignificant in appearance, were riding out to Vespignano, they were caught in a shower of rain and forced to borrow cloaks and hats from the peasants. "Well, Giotto," said the lawyer, as they trotted back to Florence clad in these old clothes and bespattered with mud from head to foot, "if a stranger were to meet you now would he ever suppose that you were the first painter in Florence?" "Certainly he would," was Giotto's prompt reply, "if beholding your worship he could imagine for a moment that you had learned your A B C!" And the novelist Sacchetti relates how the great master rode out to San Gallo one Sunday afternoon with a party of friends, and how they fell in with a herd of swine, one of which ran between Giotto's legs and threw him down. "After all, the pigs are quite right," said the painter as he scrambled to his feet and shook the dust from his clothes, "when I think how many thousands of crowns I have earned with their bristles without ever giving them even a bowl of soup!"

A more serious instance of Giotto's power of satire is to be found in his song against Voluntary Poverty, in which he not only denounces the vice and hypocrisy often working beneath the cloak of monastic perfection, but honestly expresses his own aversion to poverty as a thing miscalled a virtue. The whole poem is of great interest, coming as it does from the pen of the chosen painter of the Franciscan Order, and as showing the independence of Giotto's character.

The extraordinary industry of the man is seen by the long list of panel-pictures as well as wall-paintings which are mentioned by early writers. These have fared even worse than his frescos. The picture of 'The Commune' in the great hall of the Podestà Palace, which Vasari describes as of very beautiful and ingenious invention, the small tempera painting of the 'Death of the Virgin,' on which Michelangelo loved to gaze, in the Church of Ognissanti, Florence, the 'Madonna' which was sent to Petrarch at Avignon, and which he left as his most precious possession to his friend Francesco di Carrara, have all perished. One panel, however, described by Vasari, is still in existence – an altar-piece originally painted for a church in Pisa, and now in the Louvre.

In 1330 Giotto was invited to Naples by King Robert, who received him with the highest honor, and issued a decree granting this chosen and faithful servant all the privileges enjoyed by members of the royal household. Ghiberti tells us that Giotto painted the hall of King Robert's palace, and Petrarch alludes in one of his epistles to the frescos with which he adorned the royal chapel of the Castello dell' Uovo. "Do not fail," he writes, "to visit the royal chapel, where my contemporary, Giotto, the greatest painter of his age, has left such splendid monuments of his pencil and genius." All these works have been destroyed, and another series of frescos, which he executed in the Franciscan church of Santa Chiara, were whitewashed in the last century by order of a Spanish governor, who complained that they made the church too dark!

King Robert appreciated the painter's company as much as his talent, and enjoyed the frankness of his speech and ready jest. "Well, Giotto," he said, as he watched the artist at work one summer day, "if I were you I would leave off painting while the weather is so hot." "So would I were I King Robert," was Giotto's prompt reply. Another time the king asked him to introduce a symbol of his kingdom in a hall containing portraits of illustrious men, upon which Giotto, without a word, painted a donkey wearing a saddle embroidered with the royal crown and scepter, pawing and sniffing at another saddle lying on the ground bearing the same device. "Such are your subjects," explained the artist, with a sly allusion to the fickle temper of the Neapolitans. "Every day they seek a new master."

In 1333 Giotto was still in Naples, and King Robert, it is said, promised to make him the first man in the realm if he would remain at his court; but early in the following year he was summoned back to Florence by the Signory, and, on the twelfth of April, 1334, was appointed Chief Architect of the State and Master of the Cathedral Works. Since the death of its architect, Arnolfo, in 1310, the progress of the cathedral had languished; but now the magistrates declared their intention of erecting a bell-tower which in height and beauty should surpass all that the Greeks and Romans had accomplished in the days of their greatest pride. "For this purpose," the decree runs, "we have chosen Giotto di Bondone, painter, our great and dear master, since neither in the city nor in the whole world is there any other to be found so well fitted for this and similar tasks." Giotto lost no time in preparing designs for the beautiful Campanile which bears his name; and on the eighth of July the foundations of the new tower were laid with great solemnity. Villani describes the imposing processions that were held and the immense multitudes which attended the ceremony, and adds that the Superintendent of Works was Maestro Giotto, "our own citizen, the most sovereign master of painting in his time, and the one who drew figures and represented action in the most lifelike manner." Giotto received a salary of one hundred golden florins from the state "for his excellence and goodness," and was strictly enjoined not to leave Florence again without the permission of the Signory. In 1335, however, we hear of him in Milan, whither he had gone by order of the Signory at the urgent request of their ally Azzo Visconti, Lord of Milan. Here, in the old ducal palace, Giotto painted a series of frescos of which no trace now remains, and then hurried back to Florence to resume his work on the Campanile.

Another invitation reached him from Pope Benedict XII., who offered him a large salary if he would take up his residence at the papal court at Avignon. But it was too late; and, as an old chronicler writes, "Heaven willed that the royal city of Milan should gather the last fruits of this noble plant." Soon after his return to Florence Giotto fell suddenly ill, and died on the eighth of January, 1337. He was buried with great honor in the cathedral.

More than a hundred years later, when Florence had reached the height of splendor and prosperity under the rule of the Medici, Lorenzo the Magnificent placed a marble bust on Giotto's tomb, and employed Angelo Poliziano to compose the Latin epitaph which gave proud utterance to the veneration in which the great master was held alike by his contemporaries and by posterity:

"Lo, I am he by whom dead Painting was restored to life; to whose right hand all was possible; by whom Art became one with Nature. None ever painted more or better. Do you wonder at yon fair tower which holds the sacred bells? Know that it was I who bade her rise towards the stars. For I am Giotto – what need is there to tell of my work? Long as verse lives, my name shall endure!"

THE ART OF GIOTTO

GIORGIO VASARI – 'LIVES OF THE PAINTERS'

The gratitude which the masters in painting owe to nature is due, in my judgment, to the Florentine painter Giotto, seeing that he alone – although born amidst incapable artists and at a time when all good methods in art had long been entombed beneath the ruins of war – yet, by the favor of Heaven, he, I say, alone succeeded in resuscitating Art, and restoring her to a path that may be called the true one.

JOHN C. VAN DYKE – 'HISTORY OF PAINTING'

It would seem that nothing but self-destruction could come to the struggling, praying, throat-cutting population that terrorized Italy during the medieval period. The people were ignorant, the rulers treacherous, the passions strong; and yet out of the Dark Ages came light. In the thirteenth century the light grew brighter. The spirit of learning showed itself in the founding of schools and universities. Dante, Petrarch, and Boccaccio, reflecting respectively religion, classic learning, and the inclination toward nature, lived and gave indication of the trend of thought. Finally the arts – architecture, sculpture, painting – began to stir and take upon themselves new appearances.

In painting, though there were some portraits and allegorical scenes produced during the Gothic period, the chief theme was Bible story. The Church was the patron, and art was only the servant, as it had been from the beginning. It had not entirely escaped from symbolism. It was still the portrayal of things for what they meant rather than for what they looked. There was no such thing then as art for art's sake. It was art for religion's sake.

The demand for painting increased, and its subjects multiplied with the establishment at this time of the two powerful orders of Dominican and Franciscan monks. The first exacted from the painters more learned and instructive work; the second wished for the crucifixions, the martyrdoms, the dramatic deaths wherewith to move people by emotional appeal. In consequence painting produced many themes, but, as yet, only after the Byzantine style. The painter was more of a workman than an artist. The Church had more use for his fingers than for his creative ability. It was his business to transcribe what had gone before. This he did, but not without signs here and there of uneasiness and discontent with the pattern. There was an inclination toward something truer to nature, but as yet no great realization of it. The study of nature came in very slowly.

The advance of Italian art in the Gothic age was an advance through the development of the imposed Byzantine pattern. When people began to stir intellectually the artists found that the old Byzantine model did not look like nature. They began not by rejecting it but by improving it, giving it slight movements here and there, turning the head, throwing out a hand, or shifting the folds of drapery. The Eastern type was still seen in the long pathetic face, oblique eyes, green flesh-tints, stiff robes, thin fingers, and absence of feet; but the painters now began to modify and enliven it. More realistic Italian faces were introduced;

architectural and landscape backgrounds encroached upon the Byzantine gold grounds; even portraiture was taken up. The painters were taking notes of natural appearances. No one painter began this movement. The whole artistic region of Italy was at that time ready for the advance.

Cimabue seems the most notable instance in early times of a Byzantine-educated painter who improved upon the traditions. He has been called the father of Italian painting; but Italian painting had no father. Cimabue was simply a man of more originality and ability than his contemporaries, and departed further from the art teachings of the time without decidedly opposing them. He retained the Byzantine pattern, but loosened the lines of drapery somewhat, turned the head to one side, and infused the figure with a little appearance of life.

Cimabue's pupil, Giotto, was a great improver on all his predecessors because he was a man of extraordinary genius. He would have been great in any time, and yet he was not great enough to throw off wholly the Byzantine traditions. He tried to do it. He studied nature in a general way, changed the type of face somewhat, and gave it expression and nobility. To the figure he gave more motion, dramatic gesture, life. The drapery was cast in broader, simpler masses with some regard for line, and the form and movement of the body were somewhat emphasized through it. In methods Giotto was more knowing, but not essentially different from his contemporaries; his subjects were from the common stock of religious story, but his imaginative force and invention were his own. Bound by the conventionalities of his time, he could still create a work of nobility and power. He came too early for the highest achievement. He had genius, feeling, fancy – almost everything except accurate knowledge of the laws of nature and of art. His art was the best of its time, but it was still lacking, nor did that of his immediate followers go much beyond it technically.

Giotto, relatively to his age one of the greatest and most complete of artists, fills in the history of Italian painting a place analogous to that which seems to have been filled in the history of Greek painting by Polygnotus. That is to say, he lived at a time when the resources of his art were still in their infancy, but considering the limits of those resources his achievements were the highest possible. At the close of the Middle Age he laid the foundations upon which all the progress of the Renaissance was afterwards securely based. In the days of Giotto the knowledge possessed by painters of the human frame and its structure rested only upon general observation and not upon any minute, prolonged, or scientific study; while to facts other than those of humanity their observation had never been closely directed. Of linear perspective they possessed few ideas, and these elementary and empirical, and scarcely any ideas at all of aërial perspective or of the conduct of light and shade.

As far as painting could ever be carried under these conditions, so far it was carried by Giotto. In its choice of subjects his art is entirely subservient to the religious spirit of his age. Even in its mode of conceiving and arranging those subjects, it is in part still trammeled by the rules and consecrated traditions of the past. Thus it is as far from being a perfectly free as from being a perfectly accomplished form of art. Many of those truths of nature to which the painters of succeeding generations learned to give accurate and complete expression, Giotto was only able to express by way of imperfect symbol and suggestion. But in spite of these limitations and shortcomings, and although he had often to be content with expressing truths of space and form conventionally or inadequately, and truths of structure and action approximately, and truths of light and shadow not at all, yet among the elements over which he had control he maintained so just a balance that his work produces in the spectator less sense of imperfection than that of many later and more accomplished masters. He is one of the least one-sided of artists, and his art, it has been justly said, resumes and concentrates all the attainments of his time not less truly than all the attainments of the crowning age of Italian art are resumed and concentrated in Raphael.

In some particulars the painting of Giotto was never surpassed, – in the judicious division of the field and massing and scattering of groups, in the union of dignity in the types with appropriateness in the occupations of the personages, in strength and directness of intellectual grasp and dramatic motive, in the combination of perfect gravity with perfect frankness in conception, and of a noble severity in design with a great charm of harmony and purity in color. The earlier Byzantine and Roman workers in mosaic had bequeathed to him the high abstract qualities of their practice – their balance, their impressiveness, their grand instinct of decoration; but while they had compassed these qualities at an entire sacrifice of life and animation, it is the glory of Giotto to have been the first among his countrymen to breathe life into art, and to have quickened its stately rigidity with the fire of natural incident and emotion.

It was this conquest, this touch of the magician, this striking of the sympathetic notes of life and reality, that chiefly gave Giotto his immense reputation among his contemporaries, and made him the fit exponent of the vivid, penetrating, and practical genius of emancipated Florence. His is one of the few names in history which, having become great while its bearer lived, has sustained no loss of greatness through subsequent generations.

JOHN RUSKIN – 'GIOTTO AND HIS WORKS IN PADUA'

In the one principle of close imitation of nature lay Giotto's great strength and the entire secret of the revolution he effected. It was not by greater learning, nor by the discovery of new theories of art; not by greater taste, nor by "ideal" principles of selection that he became the head of the progressive schools of Italy. It was simply by being interested in what was going on around him, by substituting the gestures of living men for conventional attitudes, and portraits of living men for conventional faces, and incidents of every-day life for conventional circumstances, that he became great, and the master of the great.

JOHN ADDINGTON SYMONDS – 'RENAISSANCE IN ITALY'

The tale told about Giotto's first essay in drawing might be chosen as a parable: he was not found beneath a church roof tracing a mosaic, but on the open mountain, trying to draw the portrait of the living thing committed to his care. What, therefore, Giotto gave to art was, before all things else, vitality. His Madonnas are no longer symbols of a certain phase of pious awe, but pictures of maternal love. The Bride of God suckles her divine infant with a smile, watches him playing with a bird, or stretches out her arms to take him when he turns crying from the hands of the circumcising priest. By choosing incidents like these from real home life, Giotto, through his painting, humanized the mysteries of faith, and brought them close to common feeling. Nor was the change less in his method than his motives. Before his day painting had been without composition, without charm of color, without suggestion of movement or the play of living energy. He first knew how to distribute figures in the given space with perfect balance, and how to mass them together in animated groups agreeable to the eye. He caught varied and transient shades of emotion, and expressed them by the posture of the body and the play of feature. The hues of morning and of evening served him. Of all painters he was most successful in preserving the clearness and the light of pure, well-tempered colors. His power of telling a story by gesture and action is unique in its peculiar simplicity. There are no ornaments or accessories in his pictures. The whole force of the artist has been concentrated on rendering the image of the life conceived by him. Relying on his knowledge of human nature, and seeking only to make his subject intelligible, no painter is more unaffectedly pathetic, more unconsciously majestic. While under the influence of his genius we are sincerely glad that the requisite science for clever imitation of landscape and architectural backgrounds was not forthcoming in his age. Art had to go through a toilsome period of geometrical and anatomical pedantry before it could venture, in the frescos of Michelangelo and Raphael, to return with greater wealth of knowledge on a higher level to the divine simplicity of its childhood in Giotto.

In the drawing of the figure Giotto was surpassed by many meaner artists of the fifteenth century. Nor had he that quality of genius which selects a high type of beauty and is scrupulous to shun the commonplace. The faces of even his most sacred personages are often almost vulgar. In his choice of models for saints and apostles we already trace the Florentine instinct for contemporary portraiture. Yet, though his knowledge of anatomy was defective and his taste was realistic, Giotto solved the great problem of figurative art far better than more learned and fastidious painters. He never failed to make it manifest that what he meant to represent was living. Even to the non-existent he gave the semblance of reality. We cannot help believing in his angels leaning waist-deep from the blue sky, wringing their hands in agony above the Cross, pacing like deacons behind Christ when he washes the feet of his disciples, or sitting watchful and serene upon the empty sepulcher. He was, moreover, essentially a fresco-painter, working with rapid decision on a large scale, aiming at broad effects, and willing to sacrifice subtlety to clearness of expression.

The health of Giotto's whole nature and his robust good sense are every-where apparent in his solid, concrete, human work of art. There is no trace of mysticism, no ecstatic piety, nothing morbid or hysterical in his imagination. Imbuing whatever he handled with the force and freshness of actual existence, he approached the deep things of the Christian faith and the legend of St. Francis in the spirit of a man bent simply on realizing the objects of his belief as facts. His allegories of 'Poverty,' 'Chastity,' and 'Obedience,' at Assisi, are as beautiful and powerfully felt as they are carefully constructed. Yet they conceal no abstruse spiritual meaning, but are plainly painted "for the poor laity of love to read." The artist-poet who colored the virginal form of Poverty, with the briars beneath her feet and the roses blooming round her forehead, proved by his well-known *canzone* that he was free from monastic Quixotism and took a practical view of the value of worldly wealth. His homely humor saved him from the exaltation and the childishness that formed the weakness of the Franciscan revival. Giotto in truth possessed a share of that power which belonged to the Greek sculptors. He embodied myths in physical forms adequate to their intellectual meaning.

When we ask, where did Giotto get the wonderful power of expression that he shows in his work? we reply, a little from masters and a great deal from himself; but if we are asked, how did he learn to make a wall effective by color and patterns? we must answer that he worked upon traditional lines, that some of his immediate forerunners were nearly as effective as he, and that some of his remote forerunners were more effective.

When we say enthusiastically of Giotto, "There was a decorator for you! There was a muralist far more purely *decorative* than some later and even greater men!" we are thinking, not of the superiority of his drawing and composition, but of the simple flatness of his masses, free from any elaborate modeling, the lightness and purity of his color, the excellence of his silhouette and his pattern. But the essentially decorative qualities did not belong especially to Giotto; they belonged to the history and development of mural painting, to the Greeks, the Romans, the Byzantines, who had learned – centuries before St. Francis, centuries even before the Master whom Francis served, came into the world – had learned, we say, that dimly lighted interiors require flat, pure colors with little modeling.

Now nearly all the interiors of the ancient world were dimly lighted; the medieval Italian churches with their narrow lancet windows of low toned jewel-like glass were as dark as any of the antique buildings, so that the use of flat masses of pure color, the planning of an agreeable disposition of spots and of a handsome silhouette to these spots, became the canons of medieval painting. These early artists had mastered thoroughly the great controlling principle of decoration, the principle of the harmony of the painting with the surrounding architecture. Because the fourteenth century had not gone beyond this fortunate simplicity to the complexity of the fifteenth, and because it had attained to a science of draughtsmanship unknown to the thirteenth century and earlier times, we call the fourteenth century the golden age of the mural painter. The layman not infrequently supposes that this condition of things obtained because Giotto deliberately eschewed elaborate modeling, and said to mural painting, "Thus far and no farther shalt thou go!" In eight cases out of ten this misconception comes because the layman has been reading Ruskin; in the other two cases, because he has been reading Rio or Lord Lindsay. In reality, Giotto said nothing of the sort; he was a great artist, he saw and felt with simplicity and dignity; doubtless he would, under any circumstances, have modeled with restraint, but if he had known how to do so he would have put more modeling in his figures than he did.

Fifty years ago John Ruskin made Giotto the fashion. The connoisseurs of the seventeenth century, the men whose fathers had perhaps seen Raphael, had surely seen the Urbinate's great rival, made small account of the earlier painters; to them the *Giotteschi* were barbarous, rubbish. With Ruskin, however, the great son of Bondone took his place upon a throne. He sat there rightfully by virtue of the greatest talent which was given to any painter between Masaccio and the last great Greek or Roman artist of imperial days; but his ministrant swung the censer before him with such misplaced enthusiasm that the face of the great Tuscan was clouded for half a century, until modern criticism dared to say nay to the poet of the 'Stones of Venice' and the 'Modern Painters.' Ruskin never admired anything that was unworthy, though he often fiercely contemned the worthy. He saw and praised Giotto's simplicity of treatment, but how strangely he praised, how utterly he misunderstood the artist's aim and insisted upon bringing back to the marksman game that was no spoil of his! Ruskin mistook timidity for reverence, and ascribed to the painter as a deliberate choice that which was in reality forced upon him by inexperience.

The reasoning which Ruskin, Rio, and others of their school followed is peculiar. We will take as an example a fresco in which heavily draped figures stand before a city gate upon greensward. In the said greensward every little blade and leaf is made out;

there is no effect; you and I with our modern ideas would not like it at all. The critic, on the contrary, is enraptured. He cries, "Only see, Giotto has painted every leaf; he felt that everything that God made should be lovingly and carefully studied!" The draperies, on the contrary, are rather broadly and simply handled, and the author implies that it is because the artist knew that the stuffs, which were only artificial, not natural, were unworthy the careful study he had given the leaves. Such criticism as this utterly misled a portion of the English reading world for at least thirty years. The right treatment by the painter was wrongly praised by the writer. Giotto was lauded especially for leaving out that which he was incapable of putting in; his figures are but little modeled, and this slight modeling happens to be admirably suited to the kind of decoration which he was doing, but it was slight because he did not know how to carry it further. When he painted a Madonna on a panel to be seen and examined at close quarters that which was a virtue in his decoration became a fault in his easel-picture. Take the grass and draperies just mentioned; Giotto had not yet learned to paint drapery realistically, but he had the sentiment of noble composition, and he arranged his folds simply and grandly and painted them as well as he knew how, pushing them as far as he could. When he came to the grass, he found it much easier to draw a lot of little hard blades and leaves than to generalize them into an effect. He did not know how to generalize complicated detail. The drapery was one piece, and he could arrange it in a few folds, but the blades of grass were all there, and he thought he must draw every one. Ruskin, and Rio, and Lord Lindsay, all regard this incapacity as a special virtue based upon a spiritual interpretation of the relative importance of things in nature and art. They account as truth in Giotto what was really the reverse of truth. In looking at such a scene as that represented in the fresco no human being could see every blade of grass separately defined. A general effect of mass would be truth, and Giotto would have grasped it if he could have done so, but he was not yet a master of generalization.

A whole class of writers upon Christian art is like the prior in Browning's poem, who says to Fra Lippo Lippi: –

"Your business is to paint the souls of men.
"Give us no more of body than shows soul;"

but these writers, while appreciating the effect of certain qualities in Giotto and his followers, wholly misunderstood their intention. He did not leave his figures half modeled for the praise of God or for the sake of expressing soul. We might just as well say that it was for the sake of spiritual aspiration that his foreshortened feet stood on the points of their toes, or that his snub profiles were intended to suggest meekness....

It is an important fact in painting, especially in decorative painting, that in measure as an artist refines his work he may with advantage suppress one detail after another of its modeling. But this knowing what to leave out is one of the most subtle, one of the last kinds of knowledge that come to the painter. This system of elimination argues upon his part the possession of a high degree of technical accomplishment. When he can draw and paint every detail of his subject, then, and not till then, he can suppress judiciously. Great painters have thus instinctively commenced by making minutely detailed studies. Now, Giotto never made one such in his life; he did not know how. He was a beginner possessing magnificent natural gifts, still a beginner, a breaker of new paths. He drew and painted the human body exactly as well as he knew how to, leaving out elaborate modeling simply because he was unable to accomplish it. One lifetime would not have sufficed this pioneer of art for the achievement of all that he did and for the compassing of a skilful technique as well....

If we pass on to those qualities of a painter which were particular to Giotto, not merely as a muralist but as an individual man, we find that like other masters of his time he cannot yet subtly differentiate expression, but that, unlike others, his expression is more intense, more forceful, more varied. His heads have long narrow eyes, short snub noses, firm mouths, square jaws, and powerful chins; he divides them, not individually, but typically, into adolescent, adult, and aged heads. His feet are unsteady; his hands not yet understood; his draperies are for their time wonderful – simply, even grandly arranged, and if they do not express the body, at least they suggest it and echo its movements.

His animals, too small and often faulty enough, are sometimes excellent; and, like every other medieval artist, if he wanted to put in a sheep or a horse or a camel, he put it in without any misgivings as to knowledge of the subject. Neither did this architect entertain any scruples regarding architecture when he chose to paint it, and, like his fellows, he set Greek temple of Assisi, Romanesque convent, and Gothic church, all upon the same jackstraw-like legs, – that is to say, columns which made toys of all buildings, big or little. First and last and best, we see him as a miracle of compositional and dramatic capacity, and with this last quality he took his world by storm.

Men before him had tried to tell stories, but had told them hesitatingly, even uncouthly; Giotto spoke clearly and to the point. This shepherd boy, whose mountain pastures could be seen from her Campanile, taught grammar to the halting art of Florence. He taught the muse of the fourteenth century to wear the buskin, so that his followers, however confused their composition might be, were at least clear in the telling of their story. Indeed he was such a dramaturgist that men for a full hundred years forgot, in the fascination of the story told, to ask that the puppets should be any more shapely, that they should look one whit more like men and women.

HARRY QUILTER – 'GIOTTO'

The main characteristics of Giotto's style are, first, a lighter, purer tone of color than had been in use before the time of Cimabue, and a greater variety and purity of tint than had been attained by that master; second, the introduction into his compositions of a certain amount of natural detail which had been before totally neglected, and the substitution of the portraits of actual men and women for the imaginary beings that had formerly filled up the backgrounds of the Byzantine pictures; third, the power of illustrating the real meaning of his subject, not merely suggesting it as had formerly been the case; and fourth, his unrivaled dramatic power.

This dramatic power shows itself in almost every work that Giotto has left us, and even survives in the achievements of his pupils. His pictures are not scenes alone, they are *situations*. Besides their appropriateness of gesture and oneness of feeling, they possess the great characteristic of dramatic art in making the scene live before you, subduing its various incidents into one strain of meaning, yet keeping each incident complete and individual, as well as making it help the main purpose. A minor point in which the same quality shows is in the amount of emotion which this painter is capable of expressing by a single gesture – an amount so great that it occasionally runs some danger of lapsing into caricature, as is especially plain in such pictures as 'The Entombment' in the Arena Chapel. But in all his scenes Giotto has succeeded, not only in choosing the most appropriate figures for illustrating his meaning, but in seizing the very moment which is most significant.

But, after all, the main characteristic of Giotto's style is so intangible that it can only be felt, not described. This characteristic is the simple faith in which each of these compositions abounds; the feeling conveyed to the spectator that thus, and not otherwise, did the occurrence take place, and that the painter has not altered it a jot or tittle for his own purpose.

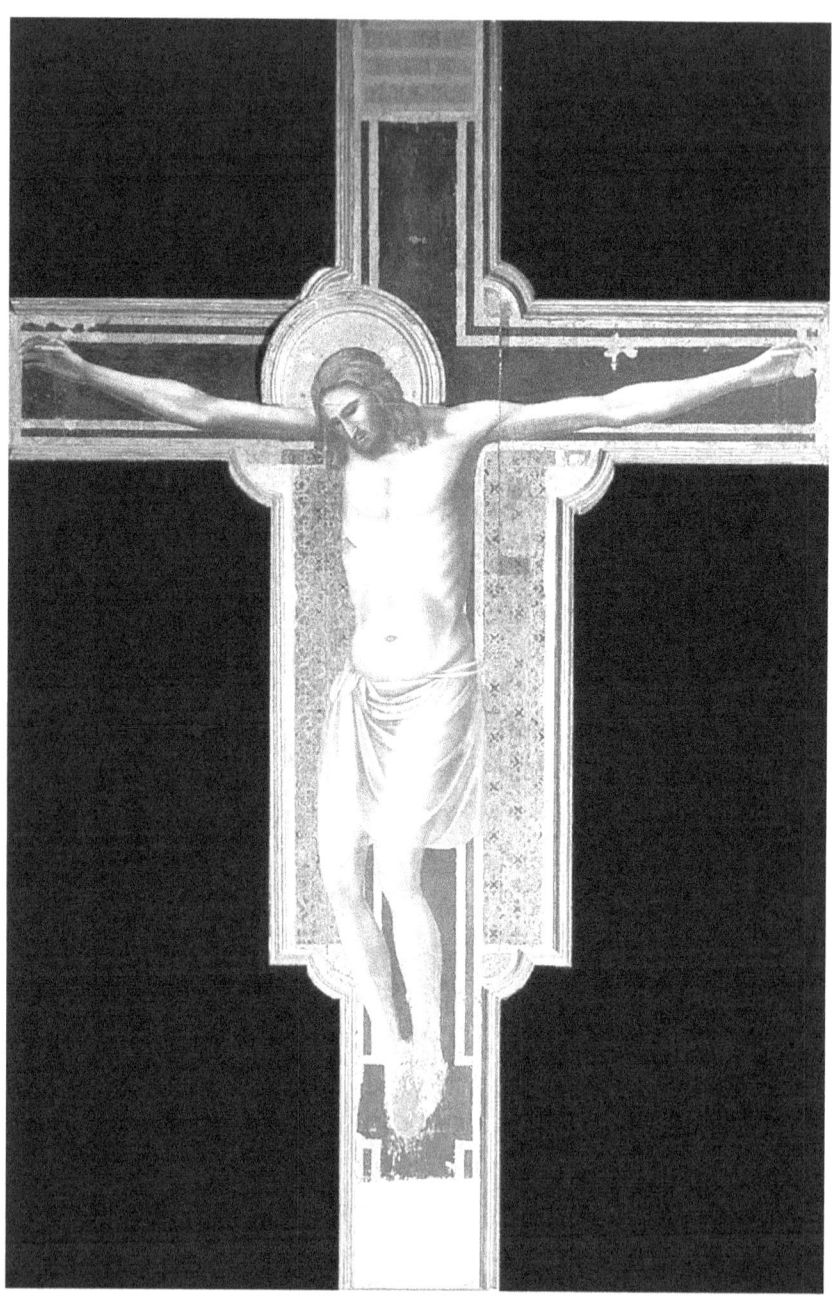

Giotto, Crucifix, 1310-17, Rimini

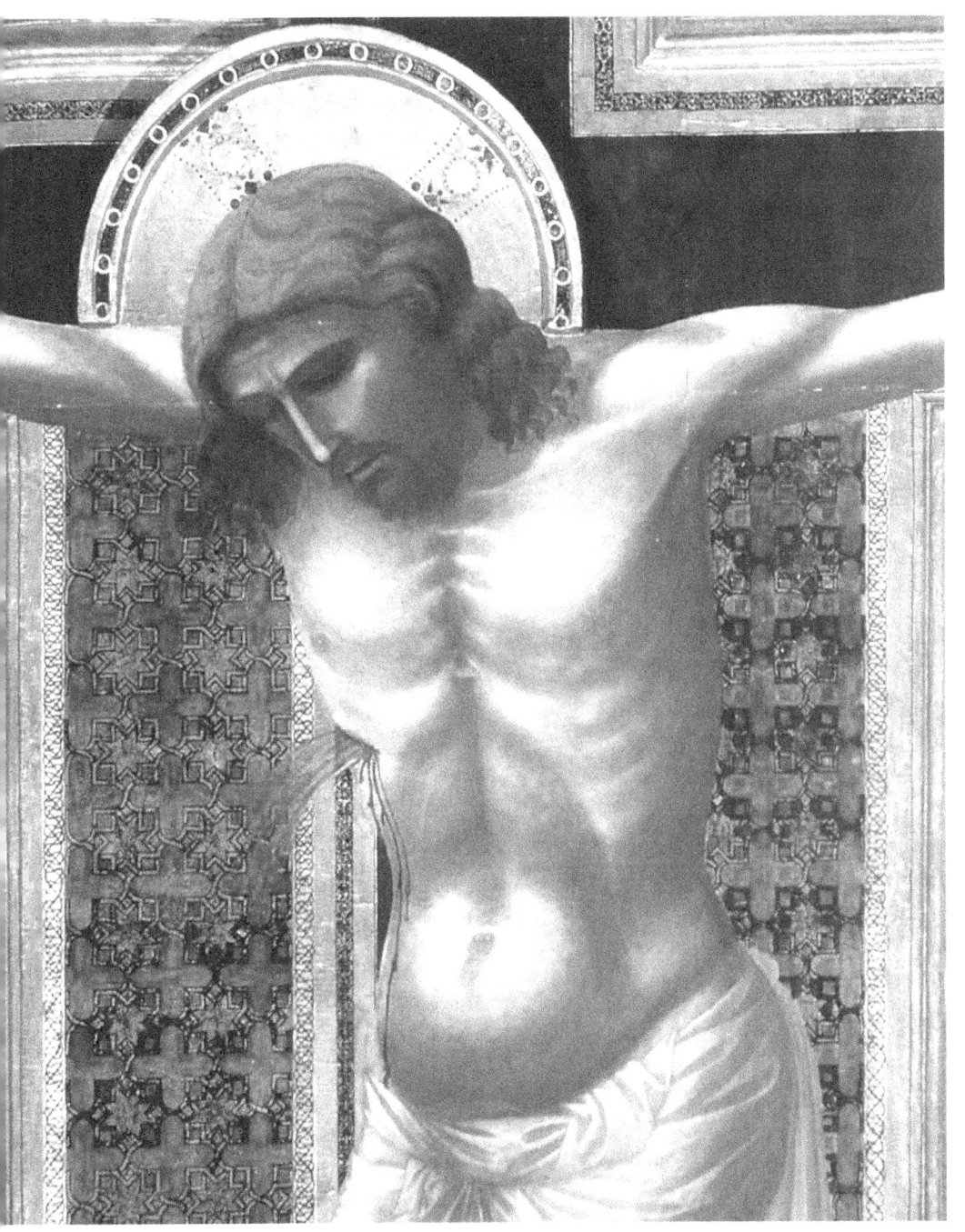

Giotto, Crucifix, 1290.

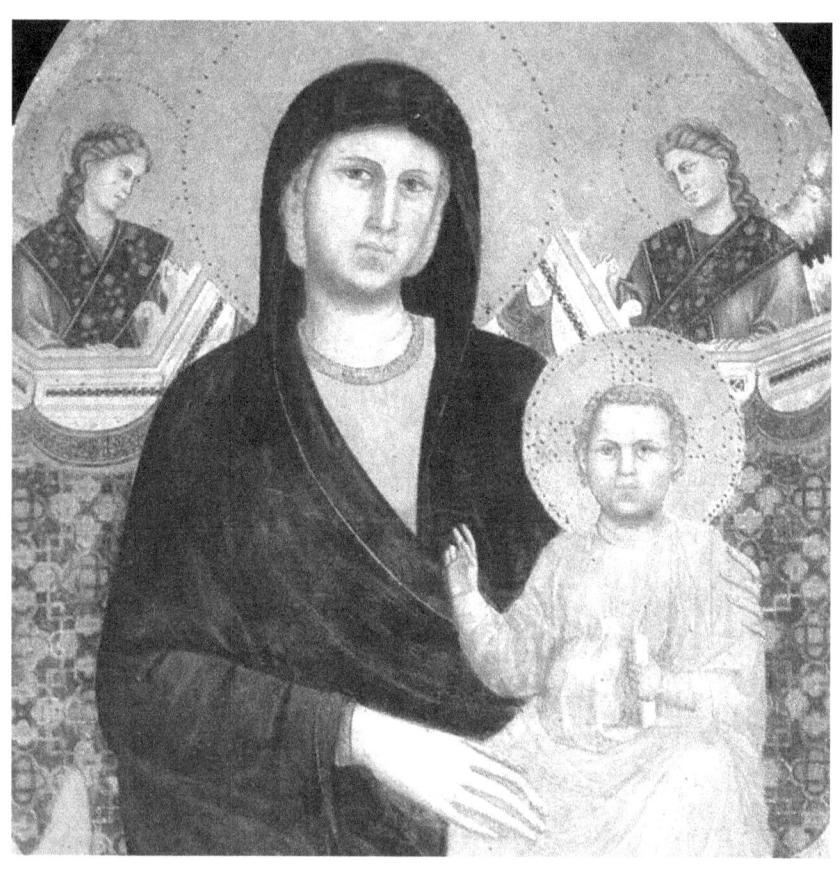

Giotto, Madonna and Child, 1290-1300, Florence

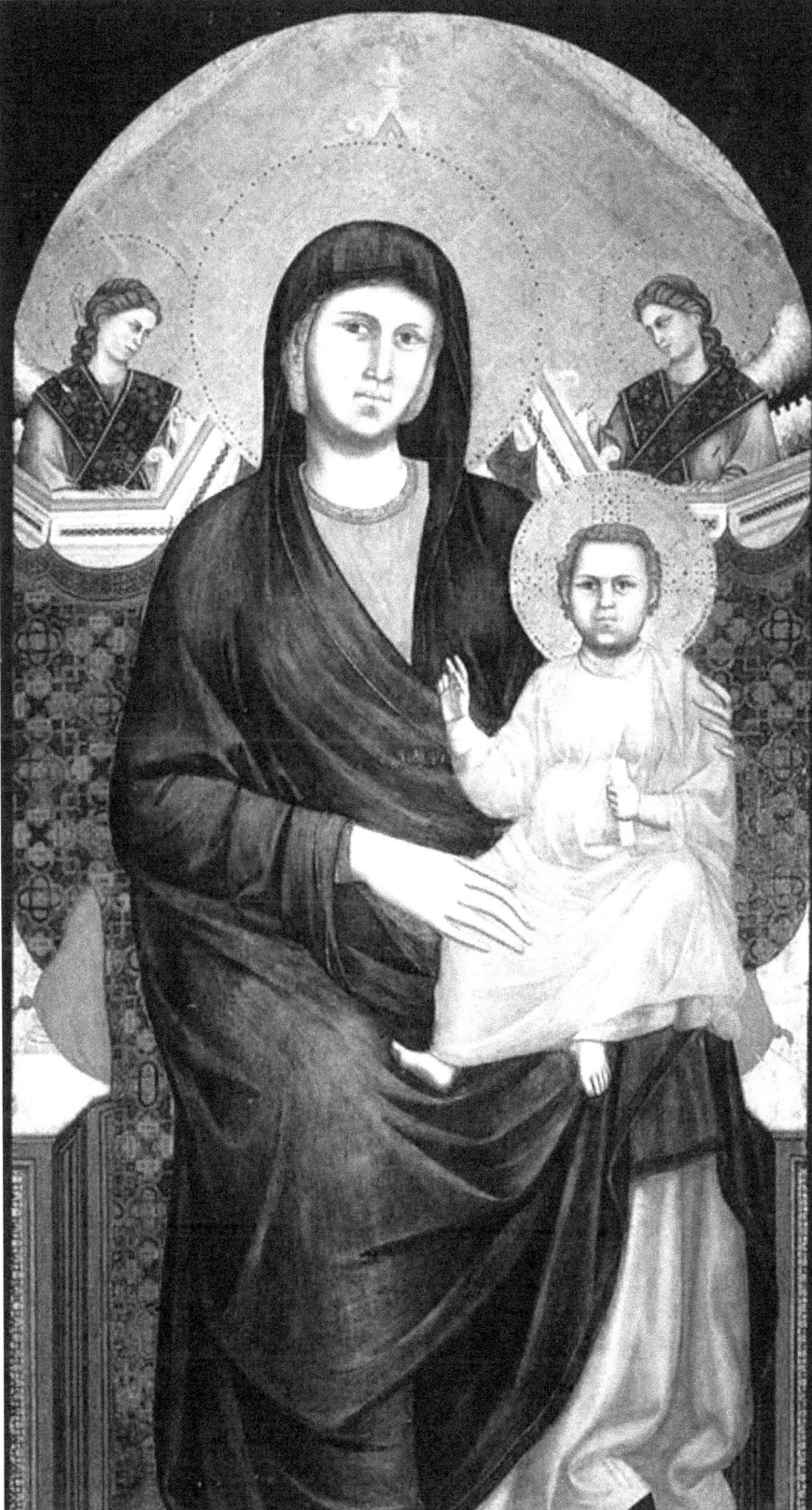

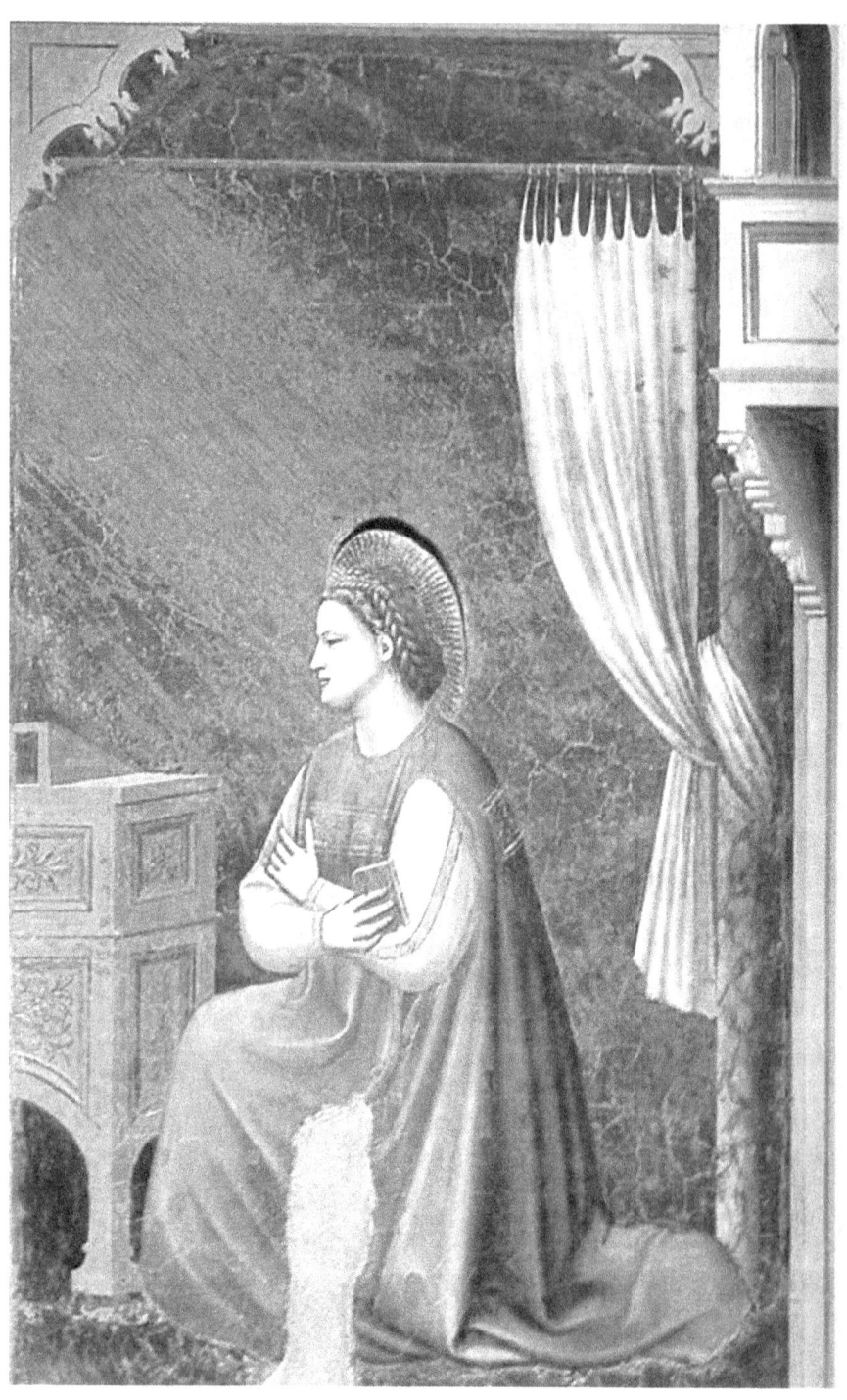

Giotto, The Annunciation – The Virgin Receiving the Message, 1306, Padua.

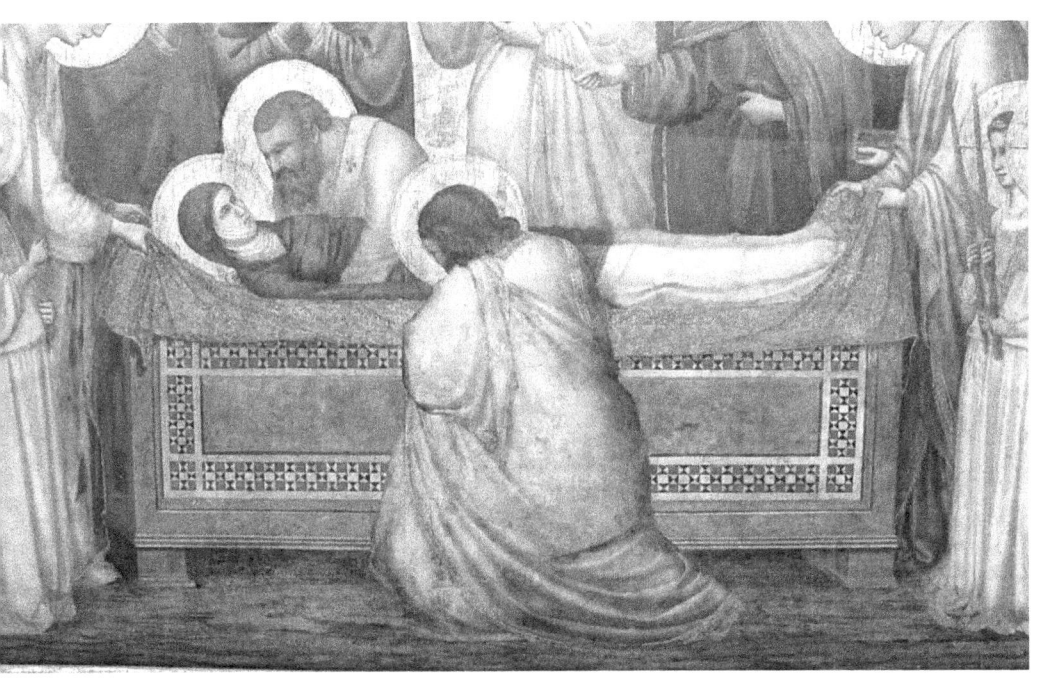

Giotto, Death of the Virgin, c. 1310, Berlin
(this page and over).

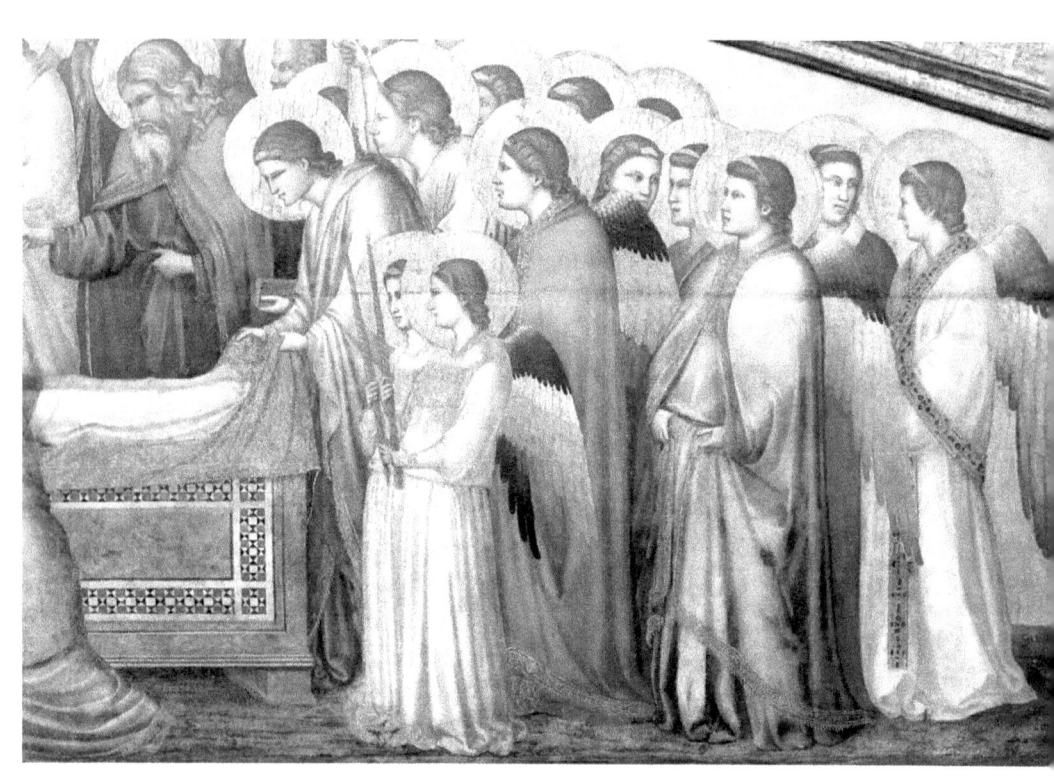

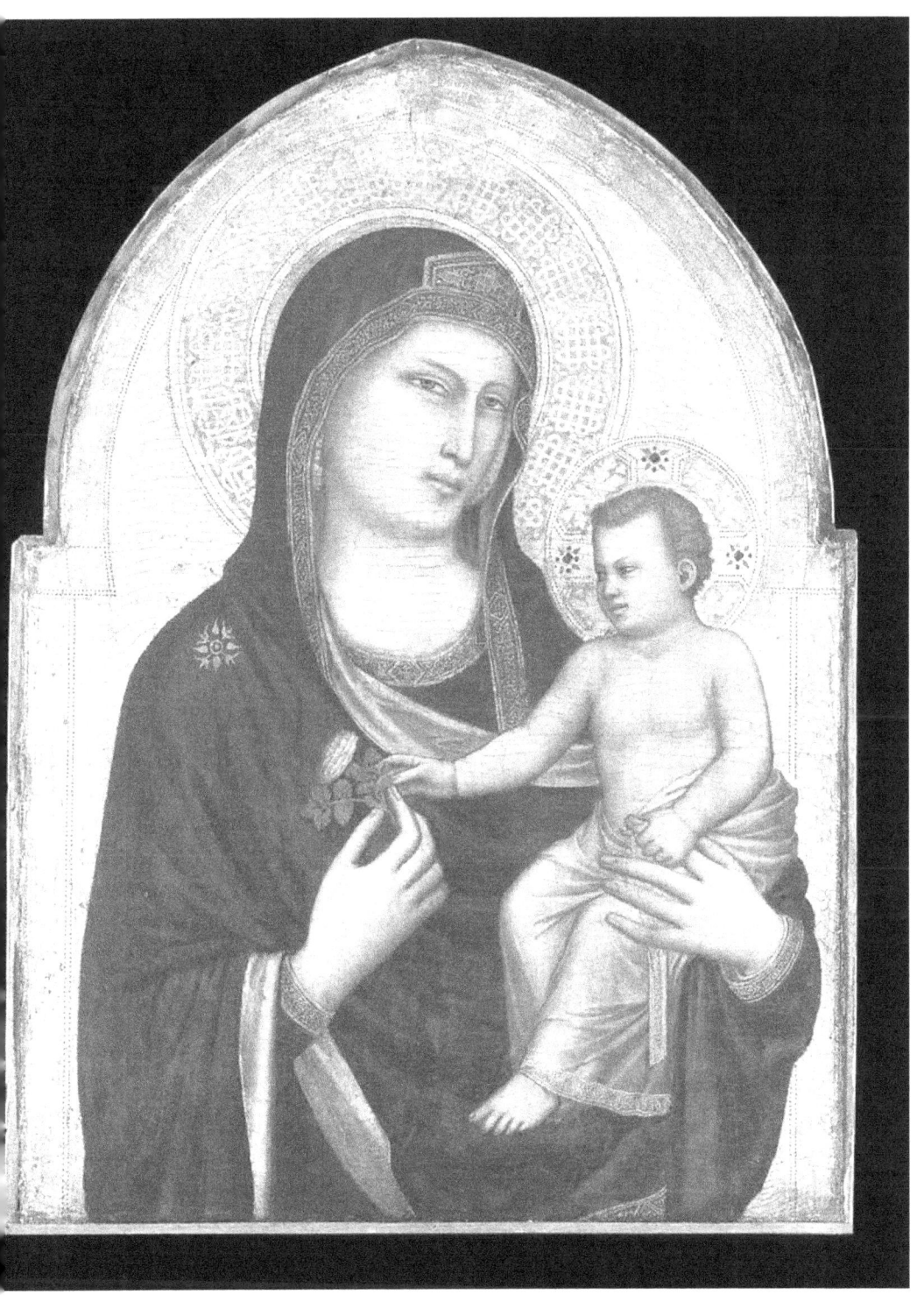

Giotto, Madonna and Child, 1320-30, Washington, DC.

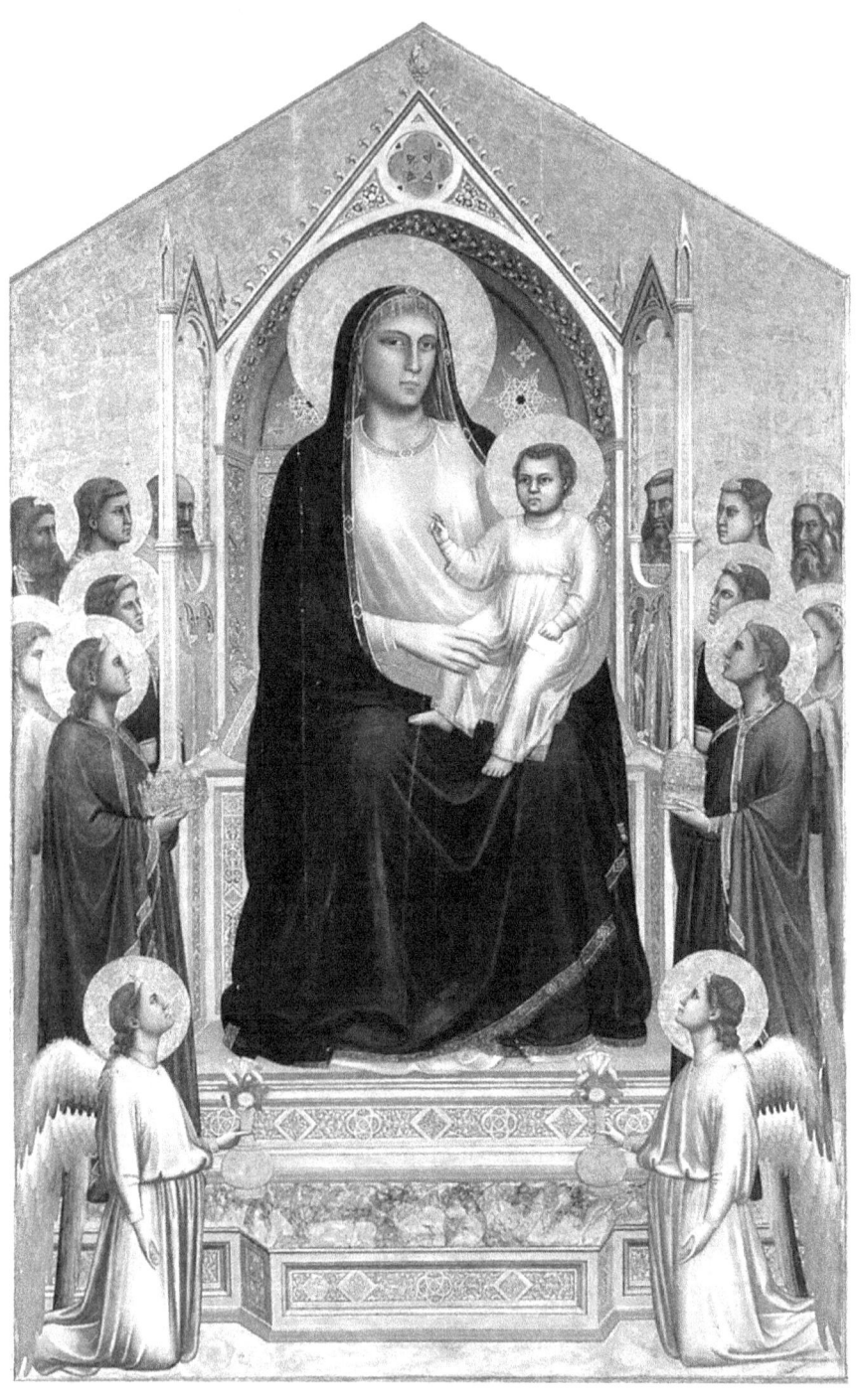

Giotto, Madonna Enthroned, c. 1310, Uffizi Gallery, Florence

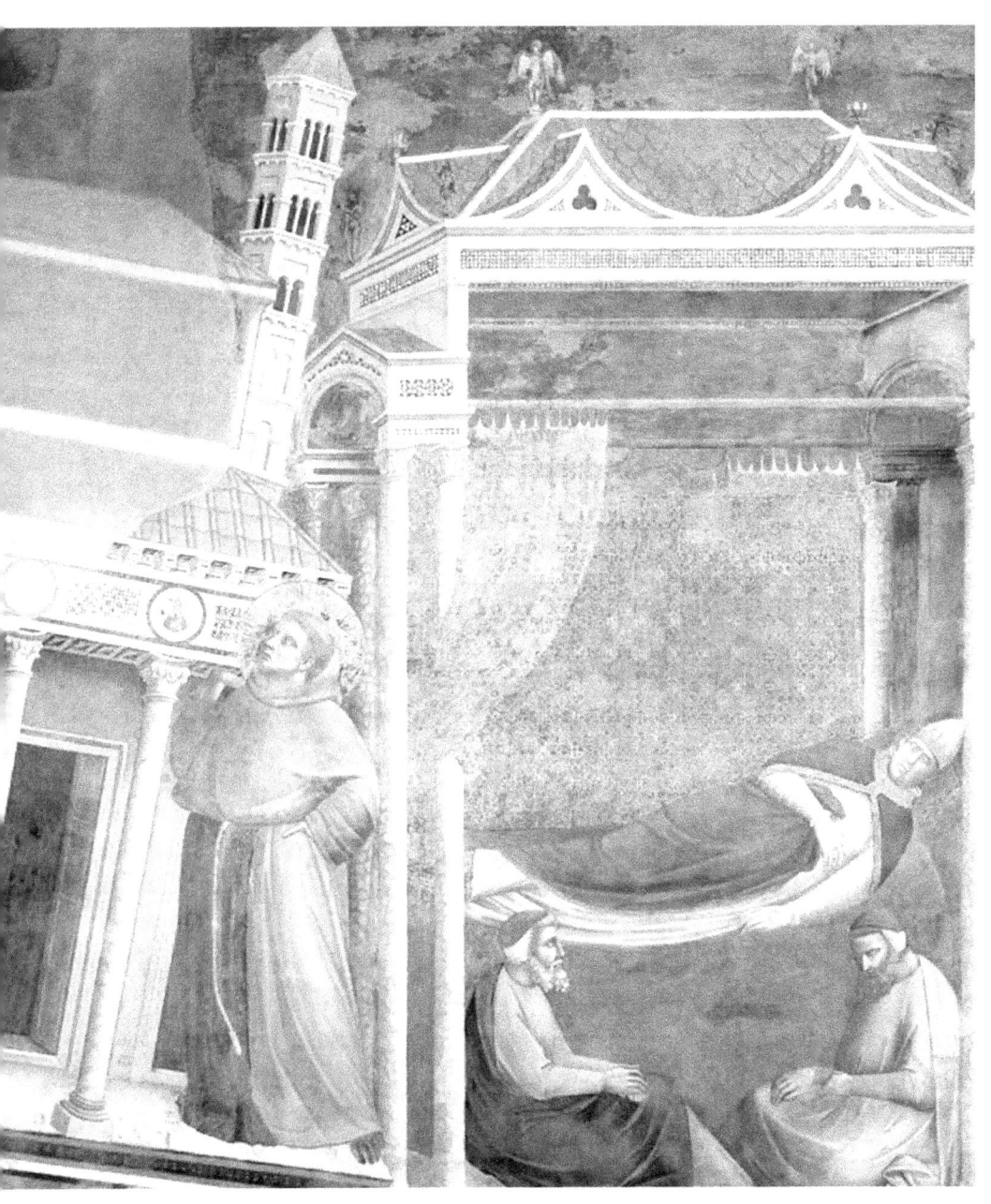

Giotto, The Dream of Innocent III, Assisi.

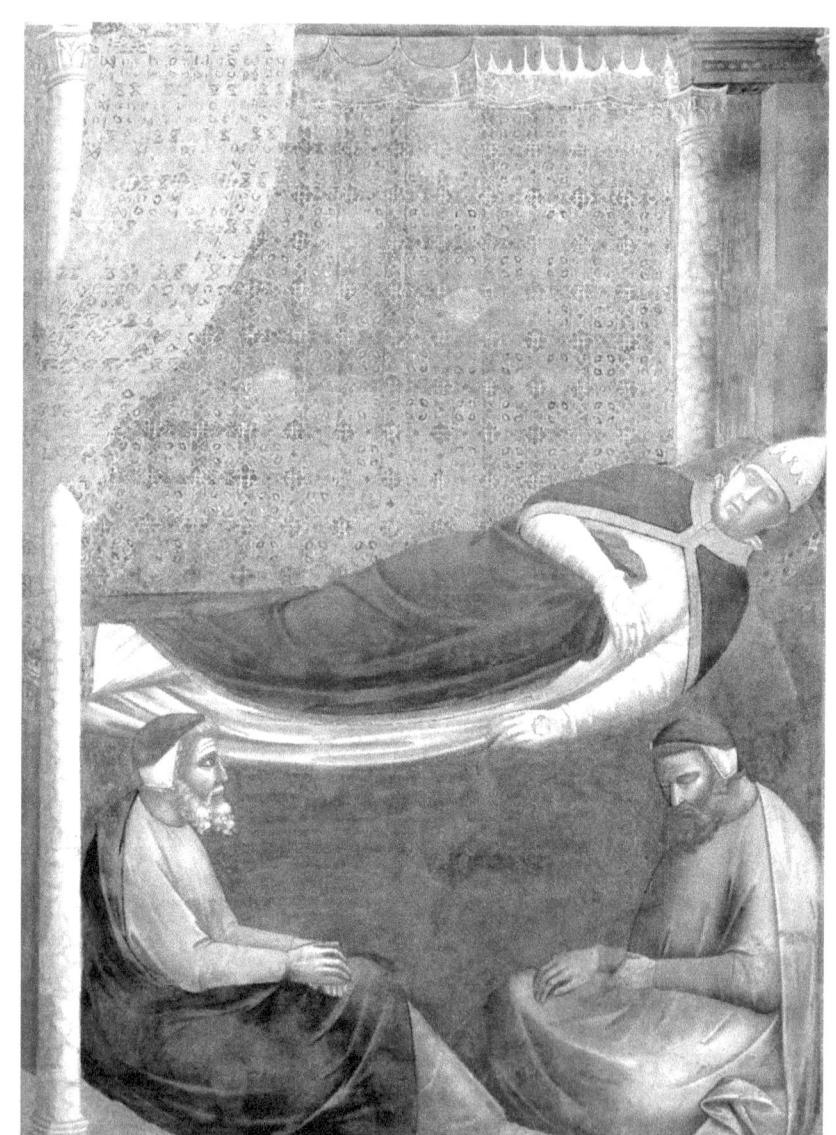

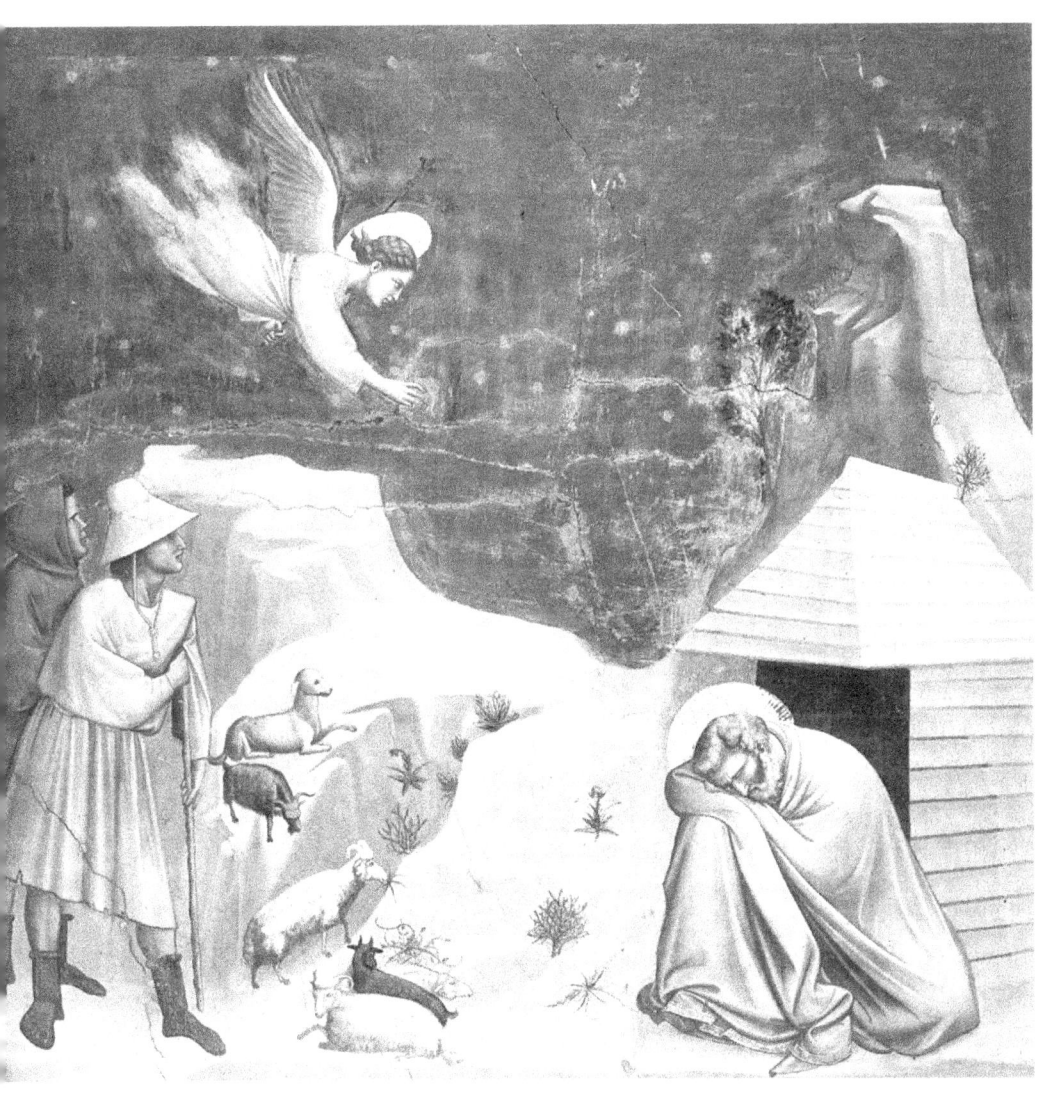

Giotto, Joachim's Dream, 1303-05, Padua.

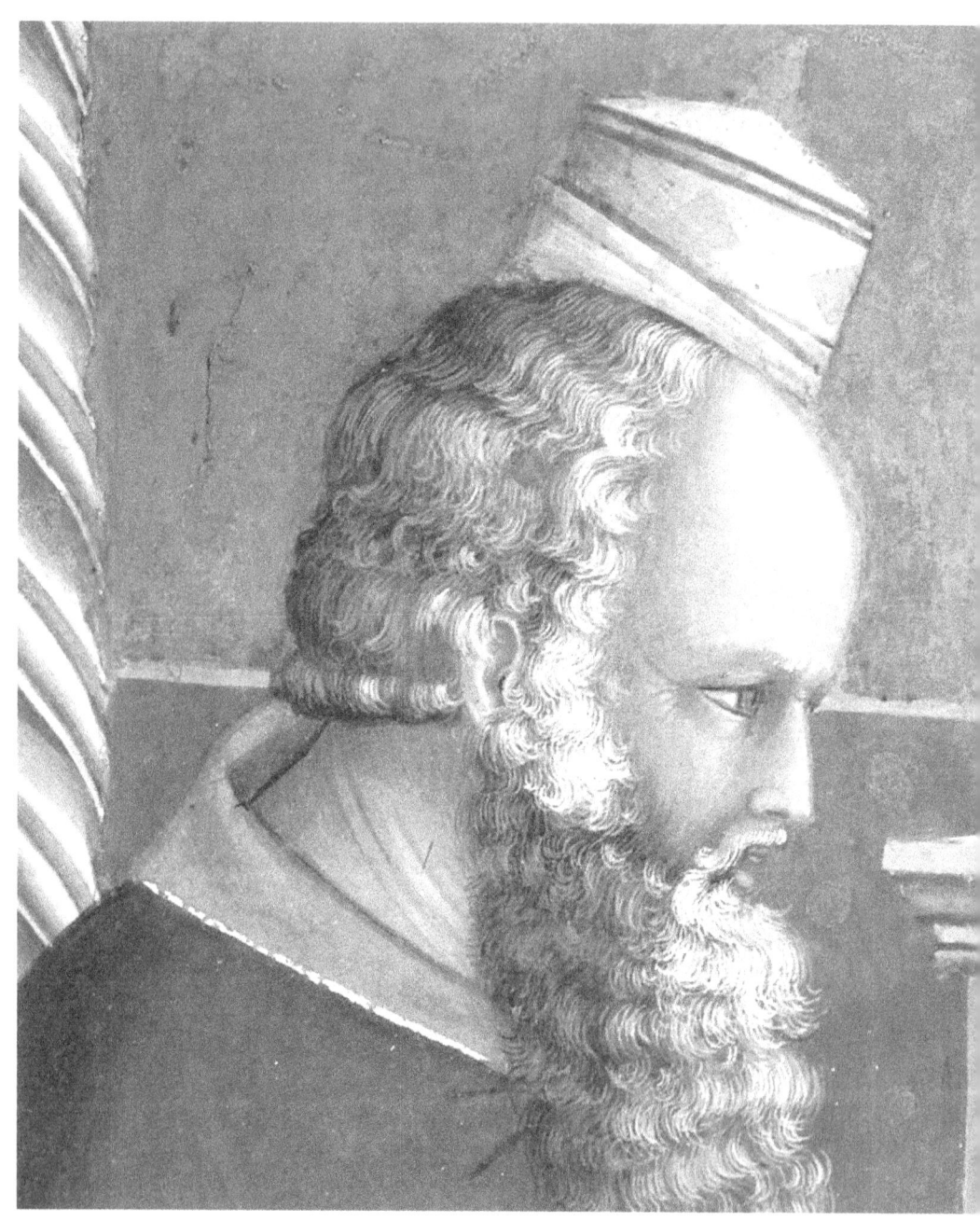

Giotto, The Expulsion of Joachim From the Temple (detail), Padua.

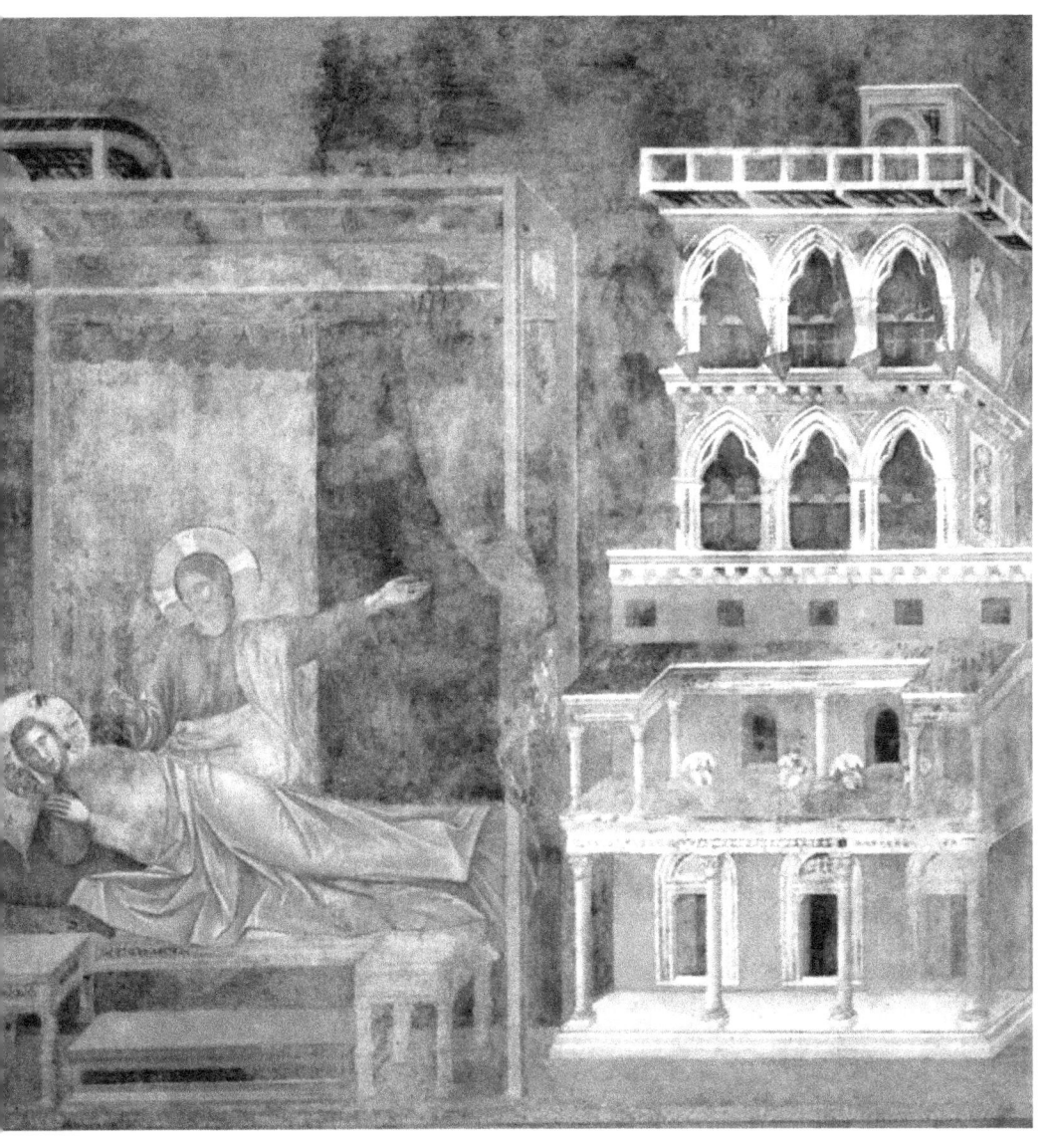

Giotto, The Dream of the Palace, The Legend of St Francis.

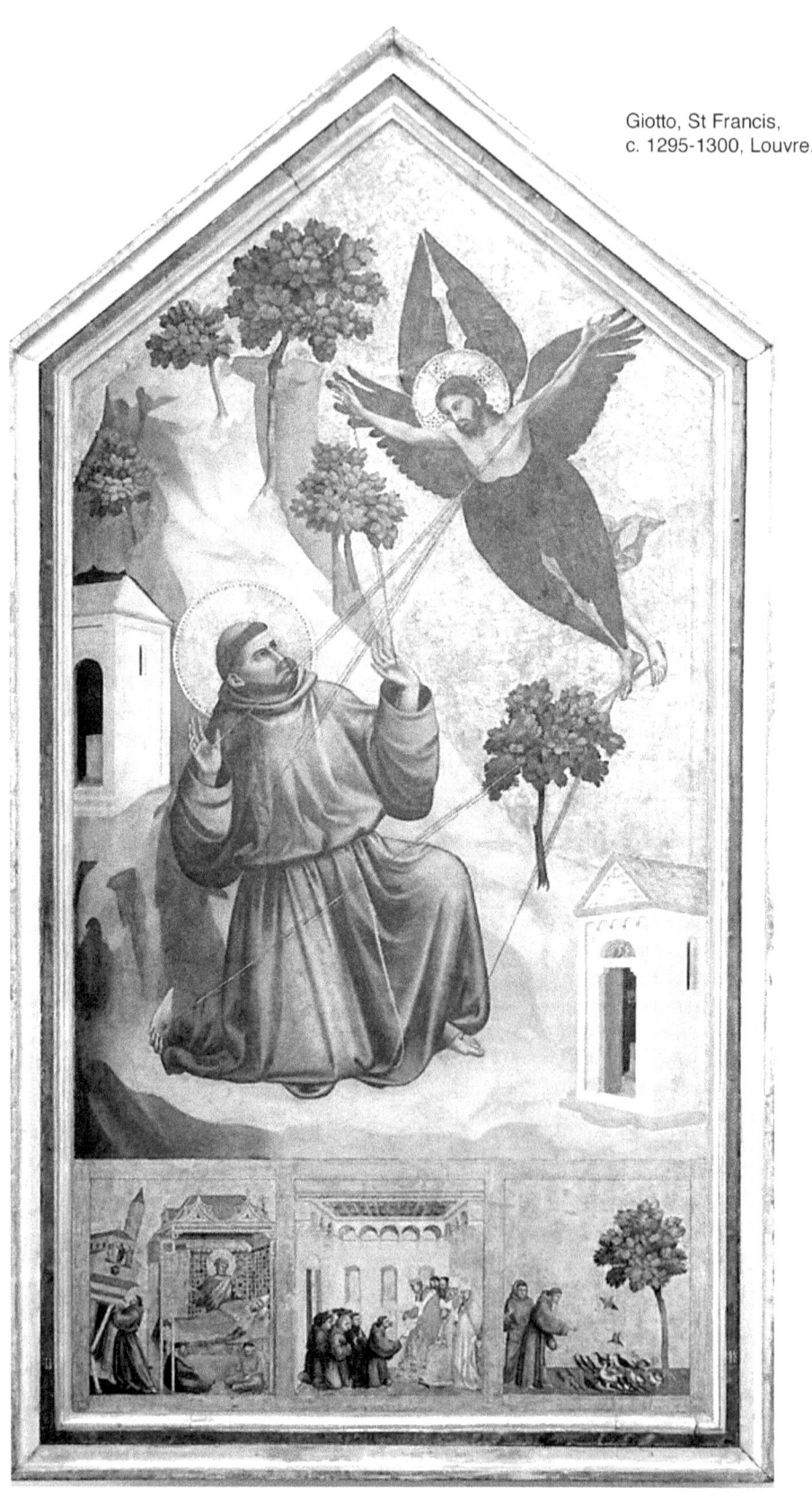

Giotto, St Francis,
c. 1295-1300, Louvre.

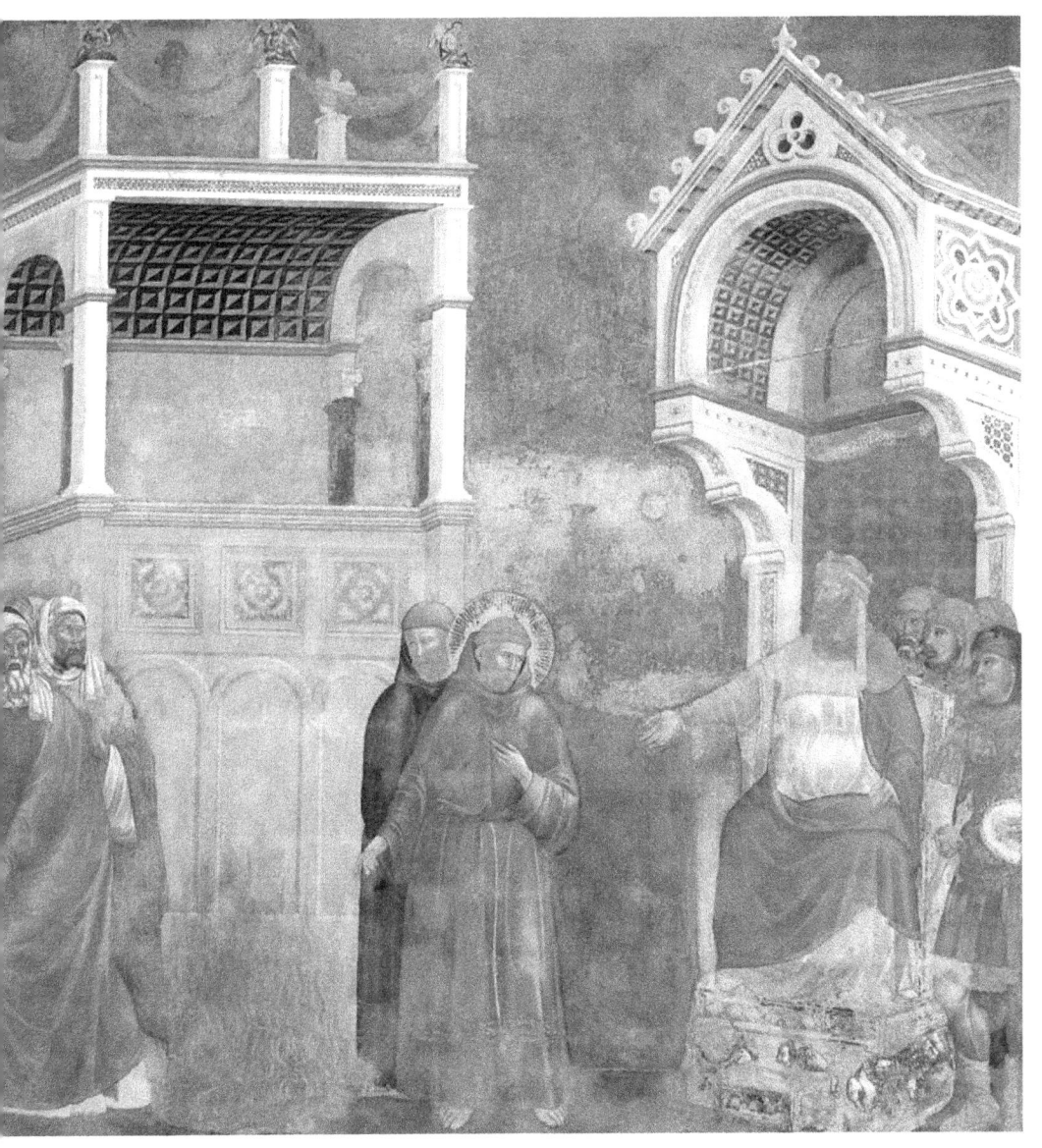

Giotto, Legend of St Francis

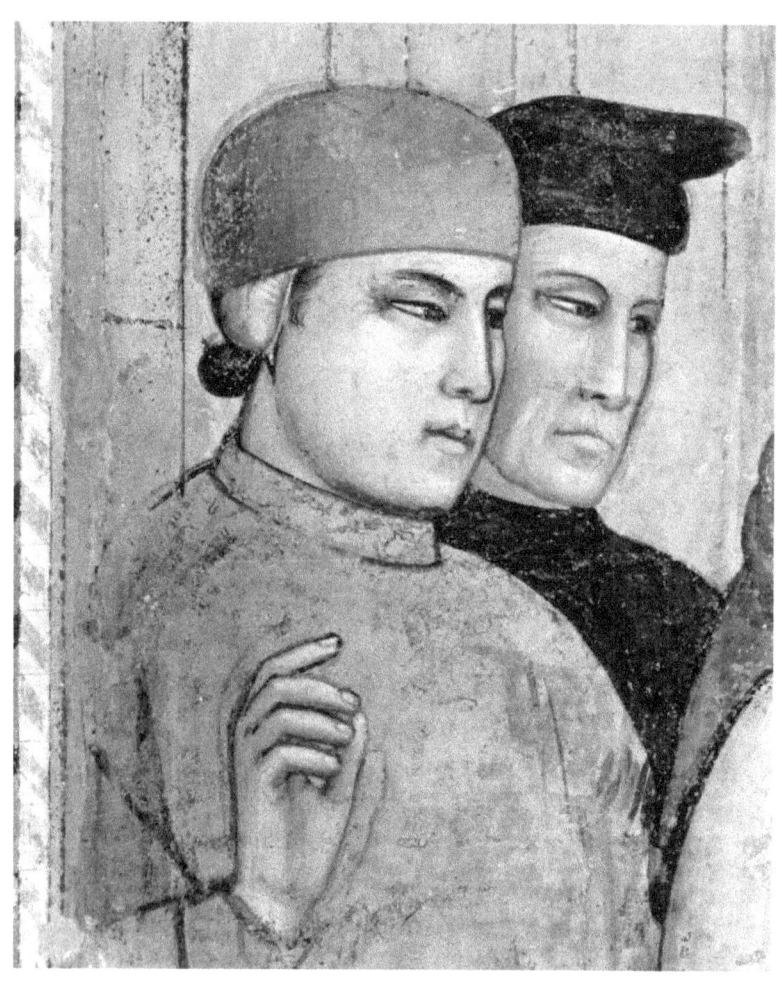

Giotto, The Death of St Francis (detail), Assisi

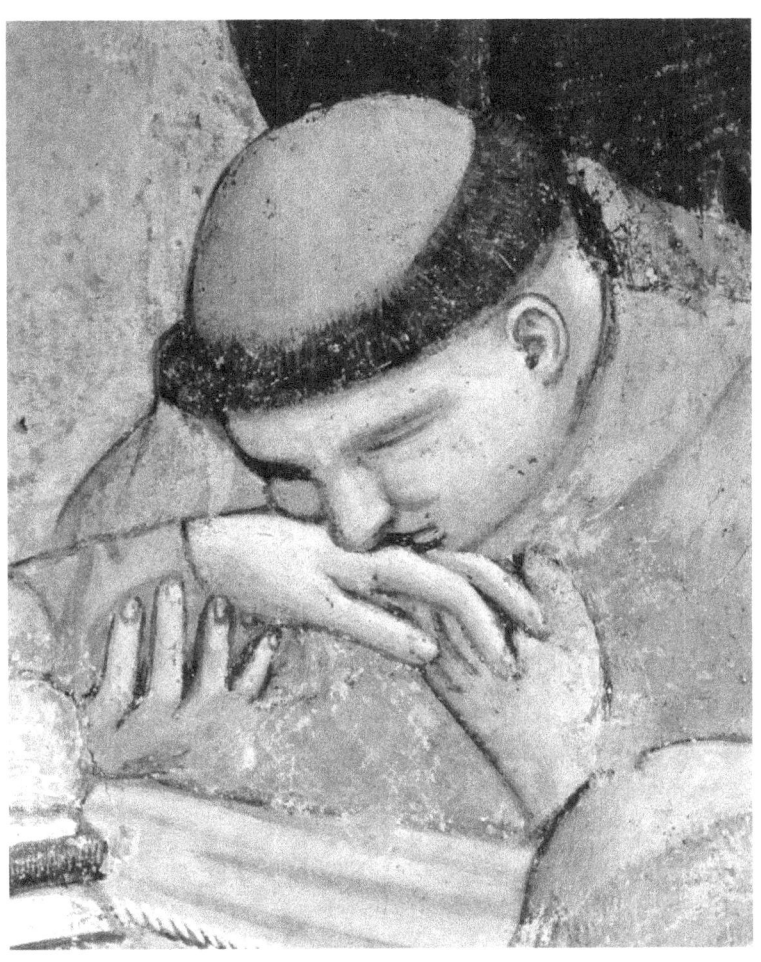

Giotto, The Death of St Francis (detail), Assisi

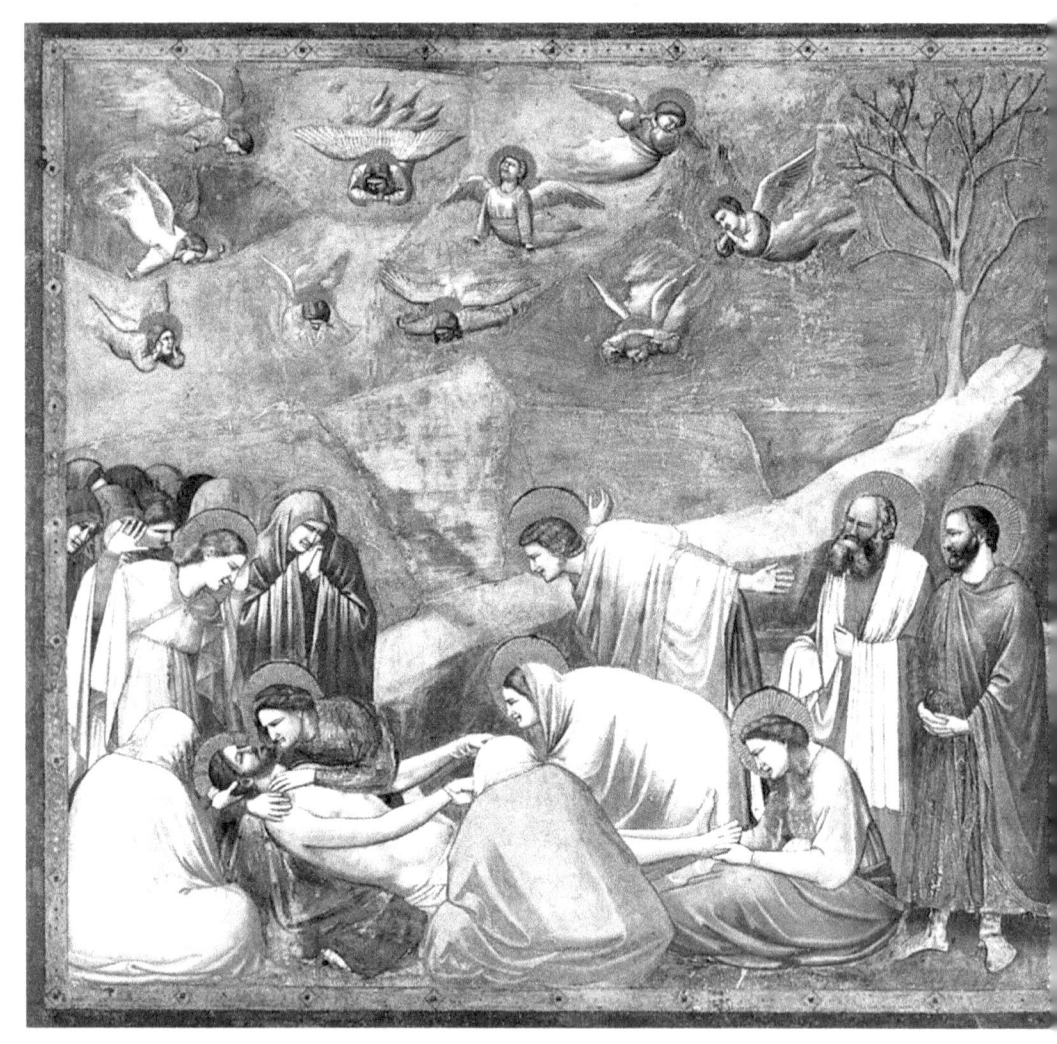

Giotto, Lamentation, 1303-06, Padua

THE WORKS OF GIOTTO

DESCRIPTIONS OF THE ILLUSTRATIONS

'MADONNA ENTHRONED'

This panel-picture, an early work, was painted for the Church of Ognissanti, Florence, and is now in the Academy of that city. Notwithstanding the fact that Giotto has adhered to the conventional composition of the Byzantine masters, there is a freshness and more lifelike appearance in this work than is observable in those of his predecessors; and in the more natural attitudes of the figures – notably in the kneeling angels – as well as in the greater freedom in the treatment of the draperies, we see the advance that he has already made in the development of art.

The Madonna, clad in a white robe and long bluish mantle, and holding the Child, whose tunic is of a pale rose color, upon her knee, is seated upon a throne placed against a gold background. The angels kneeling in front with vases of lilies in their hands are robed in white; those just above them, bearing a crown and box of ointment, are in green. Saints and angels are grouped on either side.

The color of the picture has darkened and lost much of its original freshness, and shows little of the purity of tint seen in many of Giotto's frescos.

'ALLEGORY OF POVERTY'

Among Giotto's most famous works are the four frescos which cover the arched compartments of the vaulting of the Lower Church of St. Francis at Assisi. One represents the saint enthroned in glory; the others are allegorical depictions of the three vows of the Franciscan Order, – Poverty, Chastity, and Obedience. The finest of the series is that reproduced in this plate, in which Giotto has represented the mystic marriage of St. Francis with Poverty. Hope and Love are the bridesmaids, angels are the witnesses, and Christ himself blesses the union. The bride's garments are patched, ragged and torn by brambles, children throw stones at her and mock her, and a dog barks at her; but the roses and lilies of paradise bloom about her, and St. Francis looks with love upon his chosen bride. To the left a young man gives his cloak to a beggar; on the opposite side a miser grasps his money-bag, and a richly clad youth scornfully rejects the invitation of the angel at his side to follow in the train of holy Poverty. Above, two angels, one bearing a garment and a bag of gold, the other a miniature palace – symbolical of worldly goods given up in charity – are received by the hands of the Almighty.

'ALLEGORY OF CHASTITY'

This fresco, in the Lower Church of St. Francis at Assisi, is one of the series to which that reproduced in the previous Plate also belongs. It represents the different stages of perfection in the religious life. On the left St. Francis receives three aspirants to the Franciscan Order; on the right three monks are driving evil spirits into the abyss below; and in the central group angels pour purifying water upon the head of a youth standing naked in a baptismal font. Two figures leaning over the wall behind present him with the banner of purity and shield of fortitude, and two angels standing near bear the convert's garments. The mail-clad warriors, holding lash and shield, are emblematic of the warfare and self-mortification of those who follow St. Francis. In the tower of the crenelated fortress in the background is seated Chastity, veiled and in prayer, to whom two angels bring an open book and the palm of holiness.

'NATIVITY,' 'ENTOMBMENT,' AND 'RESURRECTION'

The Arena Chapel, Padua, was built in the year 1303 by Enrico Scrovegno, a wealthy citizen of that place, upon the site of a Roman amphitheater or arena. The outside of this little building is devoid of all architectural embellishment, but any exterior bareness is more than counterbalanced by the interior, the decoration of which was, in 1305 or 1306, intrusted to Giotto, at that time the acknowledged master of painting in Italy. With the exception of the frescos in the choir, which were added by his followers in later years, all the paintings in the chapel – thirty-eight in number – are by his hand, and present a scheme of decoration that is unsurpassed even in the churches of Italy. "Though they lack the subtleties of later technical development," write Vasari's recent editors, "these frescos of the Arena Chapel, in their composition, their simplicity, their effectiveness as pure decoration, and in their dramatic force, are some of the finest things in the whole history of art, ancient or modern."

Arranged in three tiers on the side walls of the chapel, Giotto's frescos illustrate the apocryphal history of Joachim and Anna, the life of the Virgin, scenes from the life of Christ, and below, allegorical figures of the Virtues and Vices. On the entrance wall is a 'Last Judgment,' and opposite, a 'Christ in Glory.' The vaulted ceiling, colored blue and studded with gold stars, is adorned with medallions of Christ and the Virgin, saints and prophets. "Wherever the eye turns," writes Mr. Quilter, "it meets a bewilderment of color pure and radiant and yet restful to the eye, tints which resemble in their perfect harmony of brightness the iridescence of a shell. The whole interior, owing perhaps to its perfect simplicity of form and absence of all other decoration than the frescos, presents less the aspect of a building decorated with paintings than that of some gigantic opal in the midst of which the spectator stands."

'The Nativity,' reproduced in Plate IV, is the first of the second tier of frescos. It is painted almost wholly in a quiet harmony of blue and gray. Ruskin has called attention to the natural manner in which the Virgin turns upon her couch to assist in laying down the Child brought to her by an attendant, and to the figure of St. Joseph seated below in meditation. On the right are the shepherds, their flocks beside them, listening to the angels who, "all exulting, and as it were confused with joy, flutter and circle in the air like birds." On the left the ox and ass stretch their heads towards the Virgin's couch.

'The Entombment,' Plate V, is impressive in its passionate intensity. The women seated on the ground supporting the dead Christ are overwhelmed with grief, other mourners are grouped around; and in the figure of St. John with his arms extended Giotto has preserved the antique gesture of sorrow. Angels wheel and circle through the air in a frenzied agony of grief. In the background a barren hill and the leafless branches of a tree are relieved against a darkening sky.

'The Resurrection,' Plate VI, shows us the soldiers in deep sleep beside the red porphyry tomb on which two majestic, white-robed angels are seated. Mary Magdalene, in a long crimson cloak, kneels with outstretched arms at the feet of the risen Christ, who by his expressive gesture warns her, "Noli me tangere!"

This fresco and that of 'The Resurrection' are among the most impressive in the chapel, and are comparatively little injured by time and dampness.

'THE DEATH OF ST. FRANCIS'

The last in the series of eight frescos painted by Giotto in the Bardi Chapel of the Church of Santa Croce, Florence, this picture, which is by many considered his masterpiece, shows us the closing scene in the life of St. Francis of Assisi. Julia Cartwright writes of it: "The great saint is lying dead on his funeral bier, surrounded by weeping friars who bend over their beloved master and cover his hands and feet with kisses. At the head of the bier a priest reads the funeral rite; three brothers stand at the foot bearing a cross and banner, and the incredulous Girolamo puts his finger into the stigmatized side, while his companions gaze on the sacred wounds with varying expressions of awe and wonder; and one, the smallest and humblest of the group, suddenly lifts his eyes and sees the soul of St. Francis borne on angel wings to heaven. Even the hard outlines and coarse handling of the restorer's brush have not destroyed the beauty and pathos of this scene. In later ages more accomplished artist often repeated the composition, but none ever attained to the simple dignity and pathetic beauty of Giotto's design."

'THE BIRTH OF ST. JOHN THE BAPTIST'

The Peruzzi Chapel in the Church of Santa Croce, Florence, was decorated by Giotto with scenes from the lives of St. John the Baptist and St. John the Evangelist. "The frescos in this chapel have suffered greatly from repainting," writes Mr. F. Mason Perkins, "but the monumental style in which they were originally conceived is still unmistakably apparent; and they are certainly to be considered as products of the most mature period of Giotto's activity, in all probability later in date by some years at least than those in the Bardi Chapel. The fresco here reproduced represents the birth and the naming of St. John the Baptist. In one room St. Elizabeth is seen reclining on her couch and waited upon by her attendants; in an adjoining chamber Zacharias is seated writing upon a tablet the name by which the new-born child is to be called."

'THE FEAST OF HEROD'

This fresco in the Peruzzi Chapel in the Church of Santa Croce, Florence, is one of the most celebrated of Giotto's works. Herod and his guests are represented at table under a portico suggestive in its classic decorations of the later Renaissance.

Salome, a lyre in her hand, has been dancing to the music of a violin played by a youth in a striped tunic – a figure which has been the subject of enthusiastic praise from Mr. Ruskin and other writers. The girl pauses in her dance as a soldier in a Roman helmet brings the head of John the Baptist into the hall and presents it to Herod. Through an open door Salome is seen again, kneeling before her mother and bearing the charger upon which rests the head of St. John. In the distance, at the other side of the picture, we see the barred window of the tower where the Baptist has been imprisoned.

"Although little more than its outlines are left," writes Kugler, "this work unites with all Giotto's grander qualities of arrangement, grouping, and action, a closer imitation of nature than he had before attained. Seldom, even in later times, have fitter action and features been rendered that those which characterize the viol-player as he plies his art and watches the dancing Salome."

'THE RAISING OF DRUSIANA'

The story of the incident which Giotto has here portrayed has been told as follows: "When St. John had sojourned in the island of Patmos a year and a day he returned to his church at Ephesus; and as he approached the city, being received with great joy by inhabitants, lo! a funeral procession came forth from the gates; and of those who followed weeping he inquired, 'Who is dead?' They said, 'Drusiana.' Now when he heard that name he was sad, for Drusiana had excelled in all good works, and he had formerly dwelt in her house; and he ordered them to set down the bier, and having prayed earnestly, God was pleased to restore Drusiana to life. She arose up and the apostle went home with her and dwelt in her house."

"This fresco in the Peruzzi Chapel in the Church of Santa Croce, Florence, shows Giotto in all his strength and greatness," write Crowe and Cavalcaselle. "Life and animation are in the kneeling women at the Evangelist's feet, but particularly in the one kneeling in profile, whose face, while it is obvious that she cannot see the performance of the miracle on Drusiana, expresses the faith which knows no doubt. See how true are the figure and form of the cripple; how fine the movement of Drusiana; how interesting the group on the right in the variety of its movements; how beautiful the play of lines in the buildings which form the distance; how they advance and recede in order to second the lines of the composition and make the figures stand out."

A LIST OF THE PRINCIPAL PAINTINGS BY GIOTTO, WITH THEIR PRESENT LOCATIONS

ENGLAND. Alnwick Castle, Duke of Northumberland's Collection: Panel with Sposalizio, St. Francis receiving the Stigmata, etc. –

FRANCE. Paris, Louvre: St. Francis receiving the Stigmata –

GERMANY. Munich Gallery: Small Panels of Crucifixion, Last Supper, etc. –

ITALY. Assisi, Church of St. Francis, upper church: Frescos from the Life of St. Francis; LOWER CHURCH: Allegorical Frescos of Chastity, Obedience, and Poverty, and St. Francis in Glory; Frescos from the Lives of Christ and the Virgin, and Miracles of St. Francis – Bologna, Academy: Saints and Angels – Florence, Academy: Madonna Enthroned – Florence, Church of Santa Croce, Bardi Chapel: Frescos from the Life of St. Francis; Peruzzi Chapel: Frescos from the Lives of St. John the Baptist and St. John the Evangelist – Padua, Arena Chapel: Frescos from the Lives of Christ and the Virgin; Last Judgment; Christ in Glory; Allegorical Figures of the Virtues and Vices; sacristy: Crucifix – Padua, Church of Sant' Antonio: Frescos of Saints – Rome, Church of San Giovanni Laterano: Pope Boniface VIII. proclaiming the Jubilee –

UNITED STATES. Boston, Mrs. J. L. Gardner's Collection: Presentation in the Temple.

On the following pages are illustrations of some of the contemporaries of Giotto.

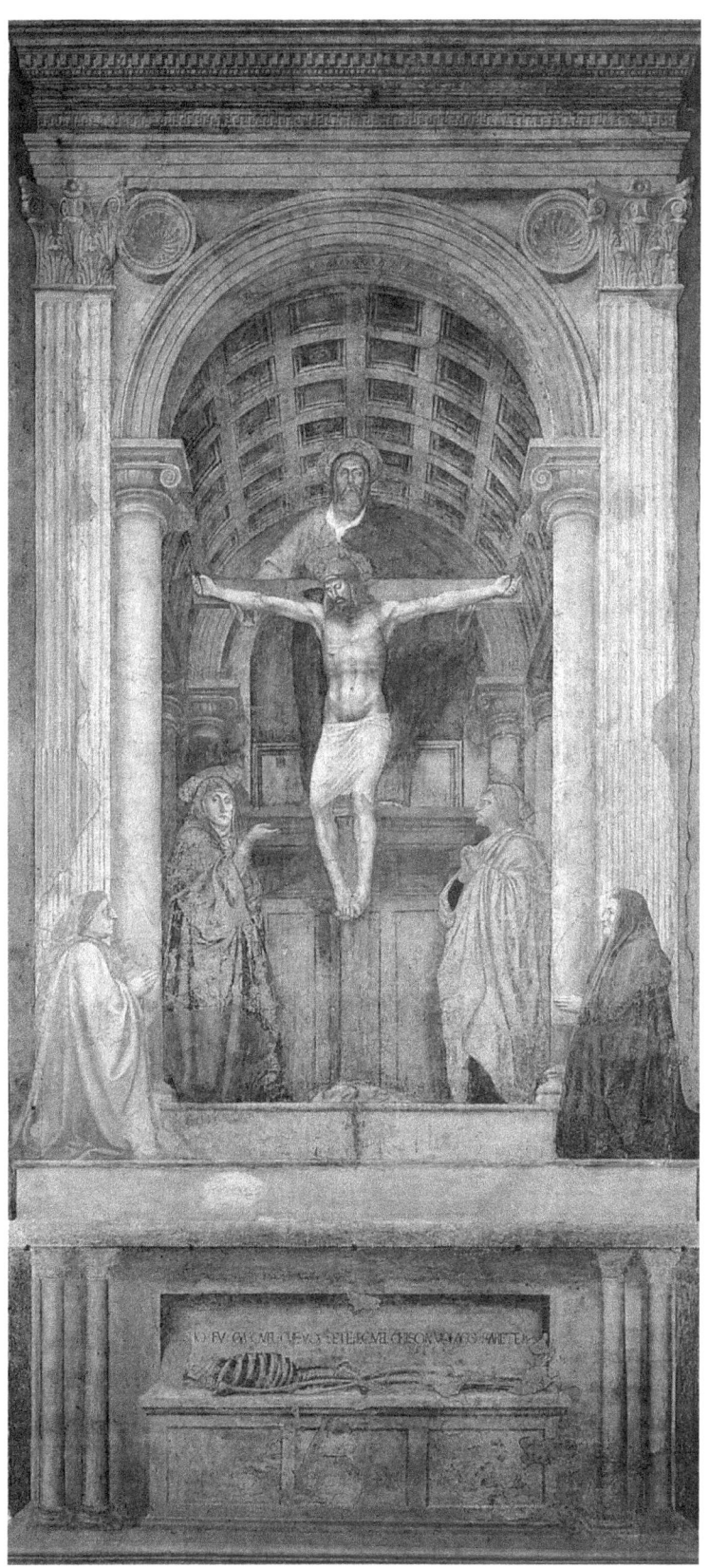

Tomasso Masaccio,
The Trinity,
1426-28, Florence

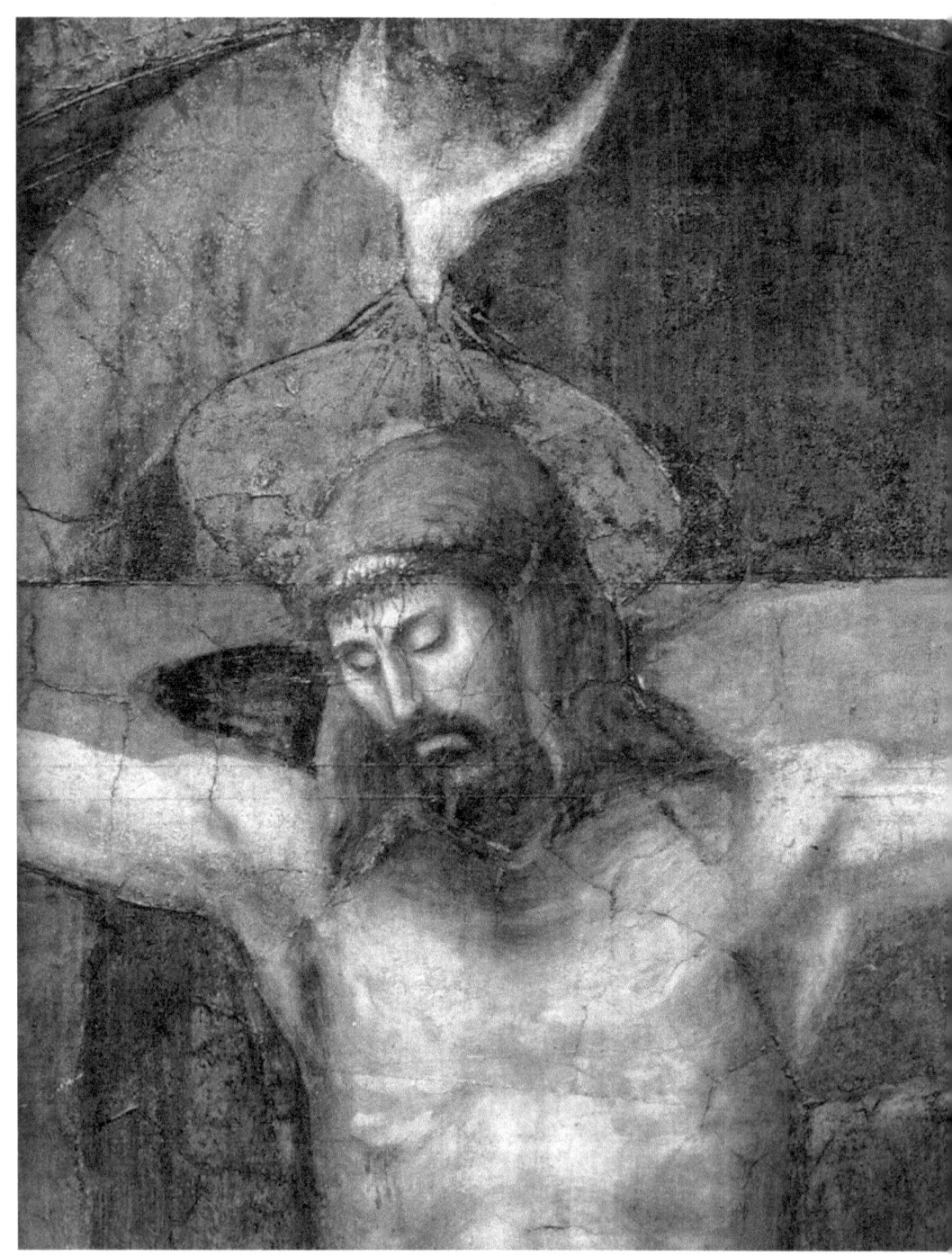

Tomasso Masaccio, The Trinity, detail

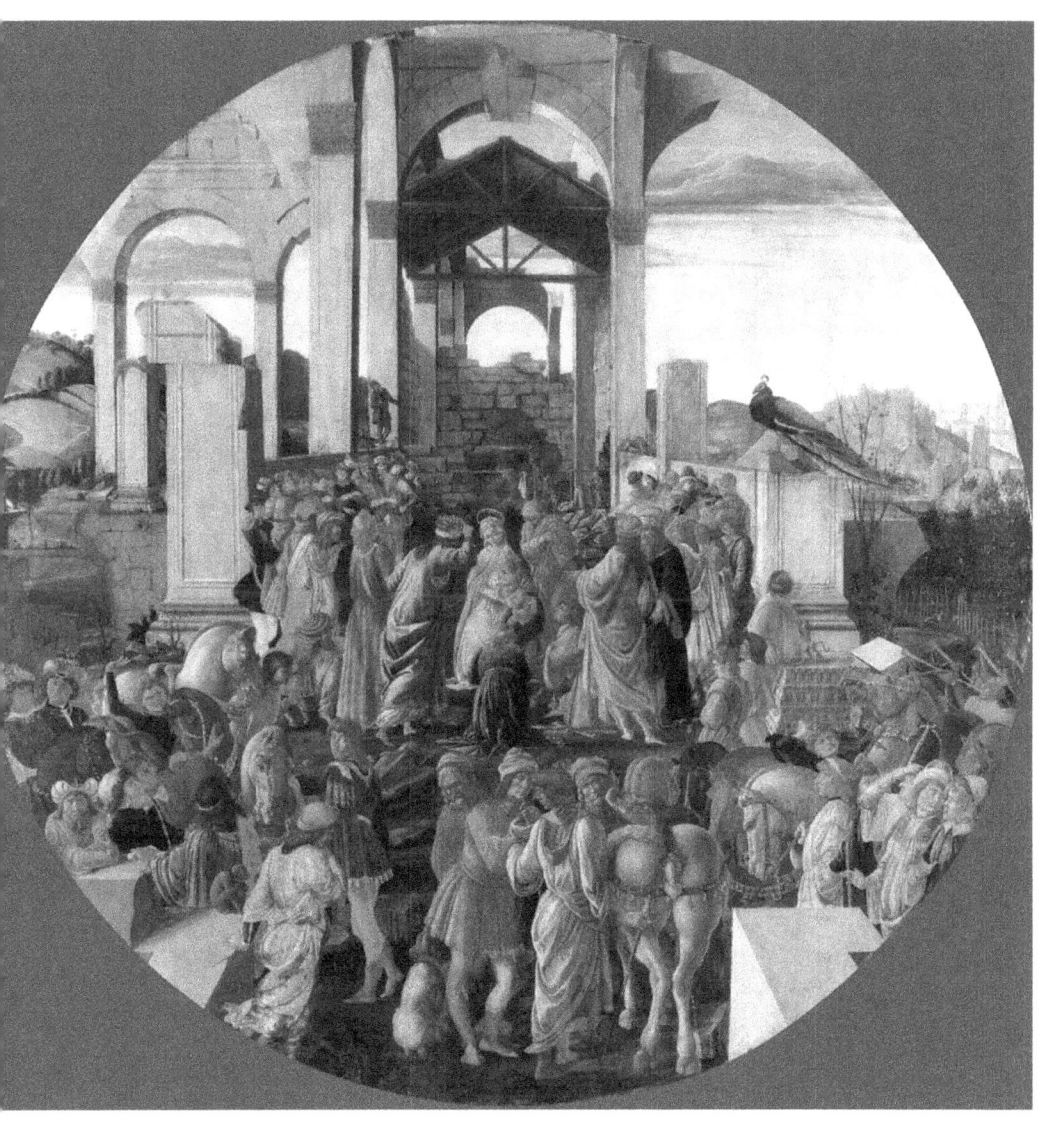

Sandro Botticelli, Adorazione dei Magi, National Gallery, London, 1470-75

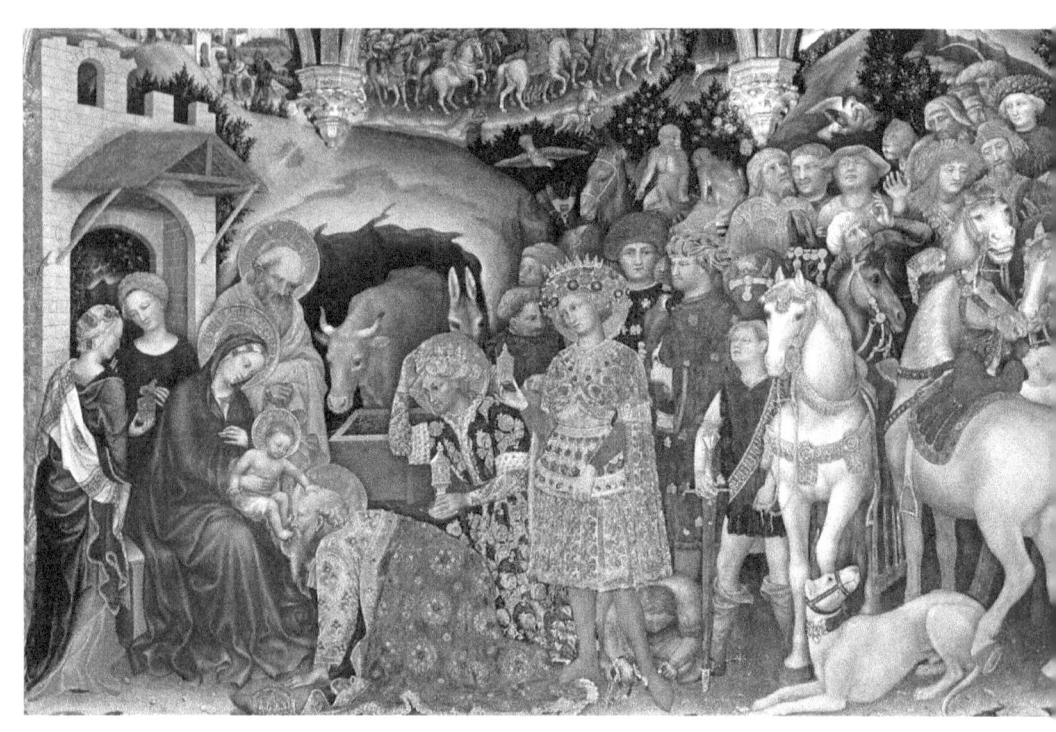

Gentile da Fabriano, Adorazione dei Magi, 1423, Uffizi Gallery

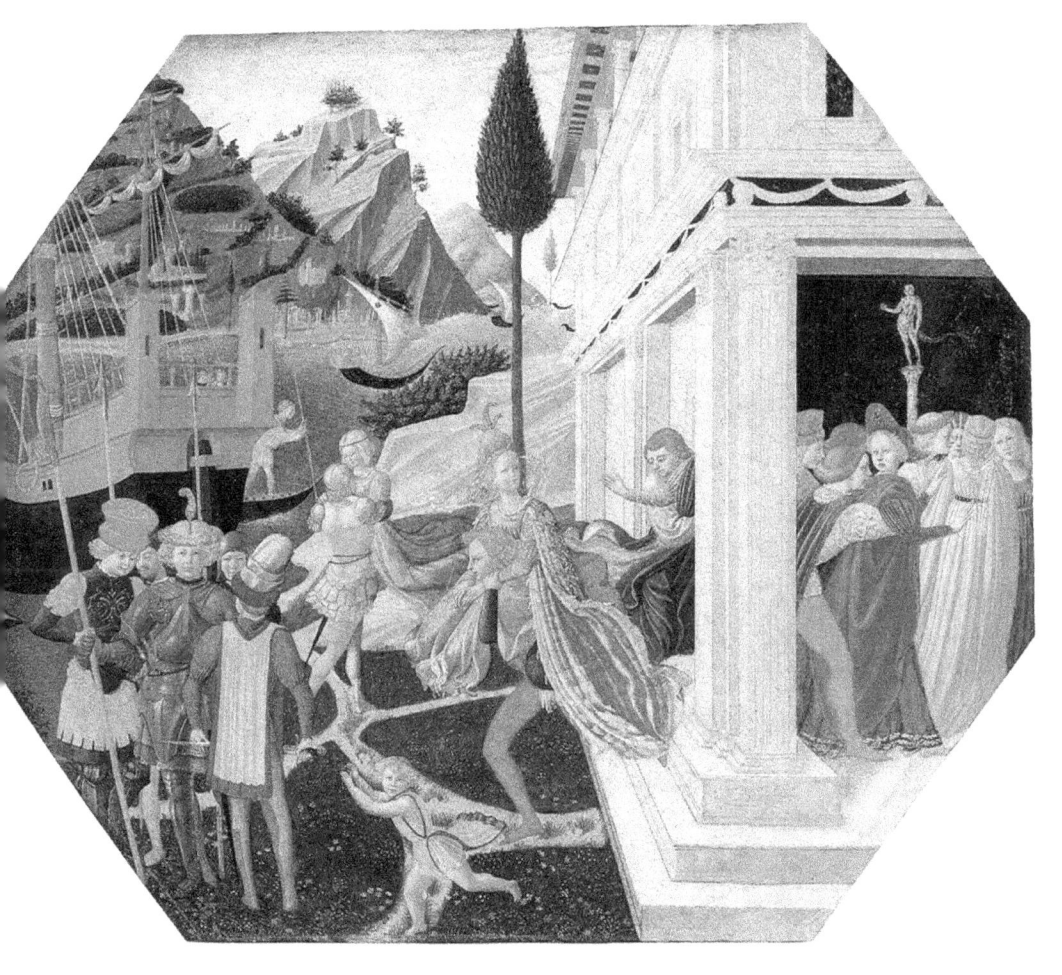

Benozzo Gozzoli, The Rape of Helen, London

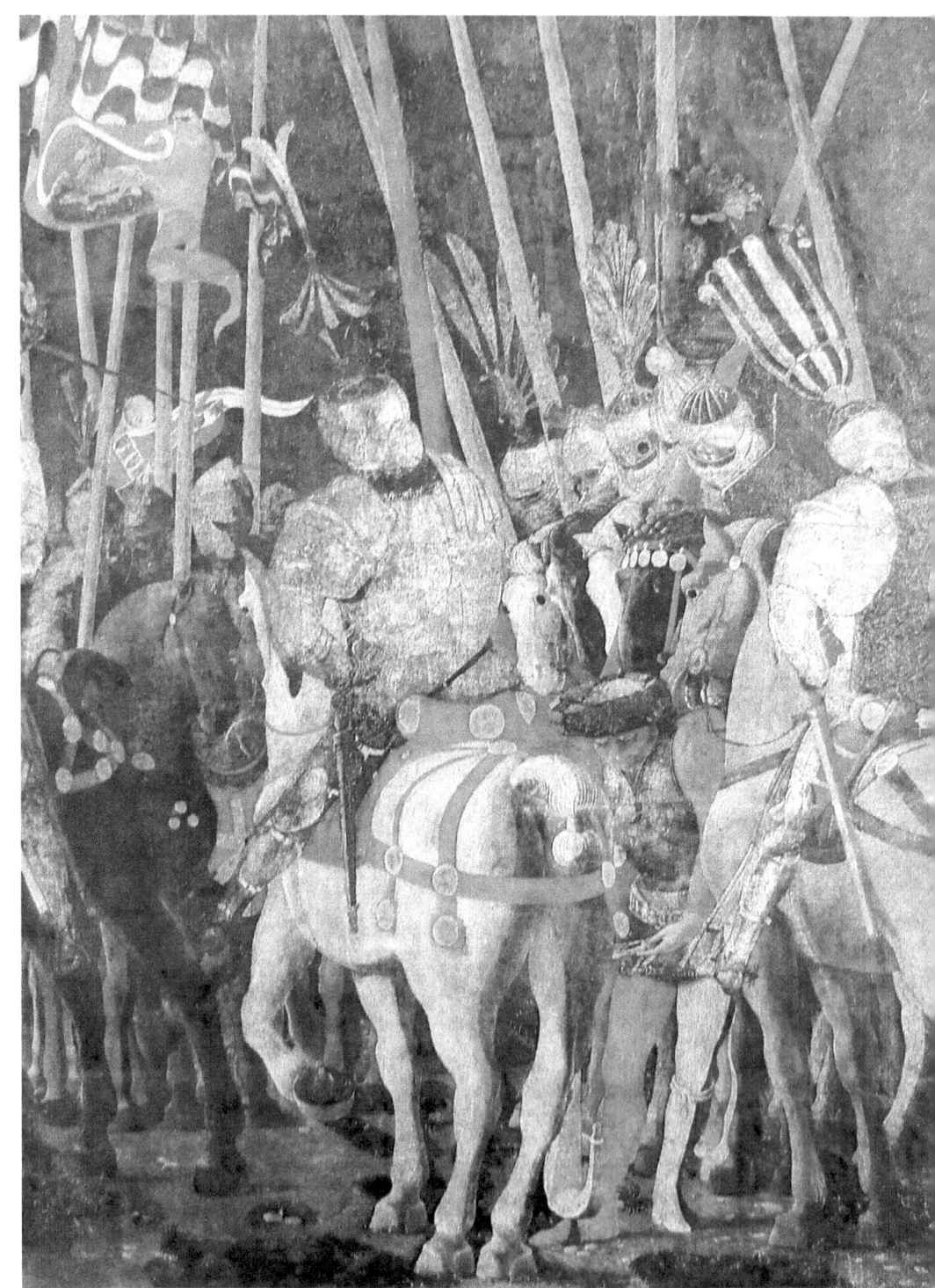

Paolo Uccello, Battle of San Romano, 1456-60, Loure, Paris

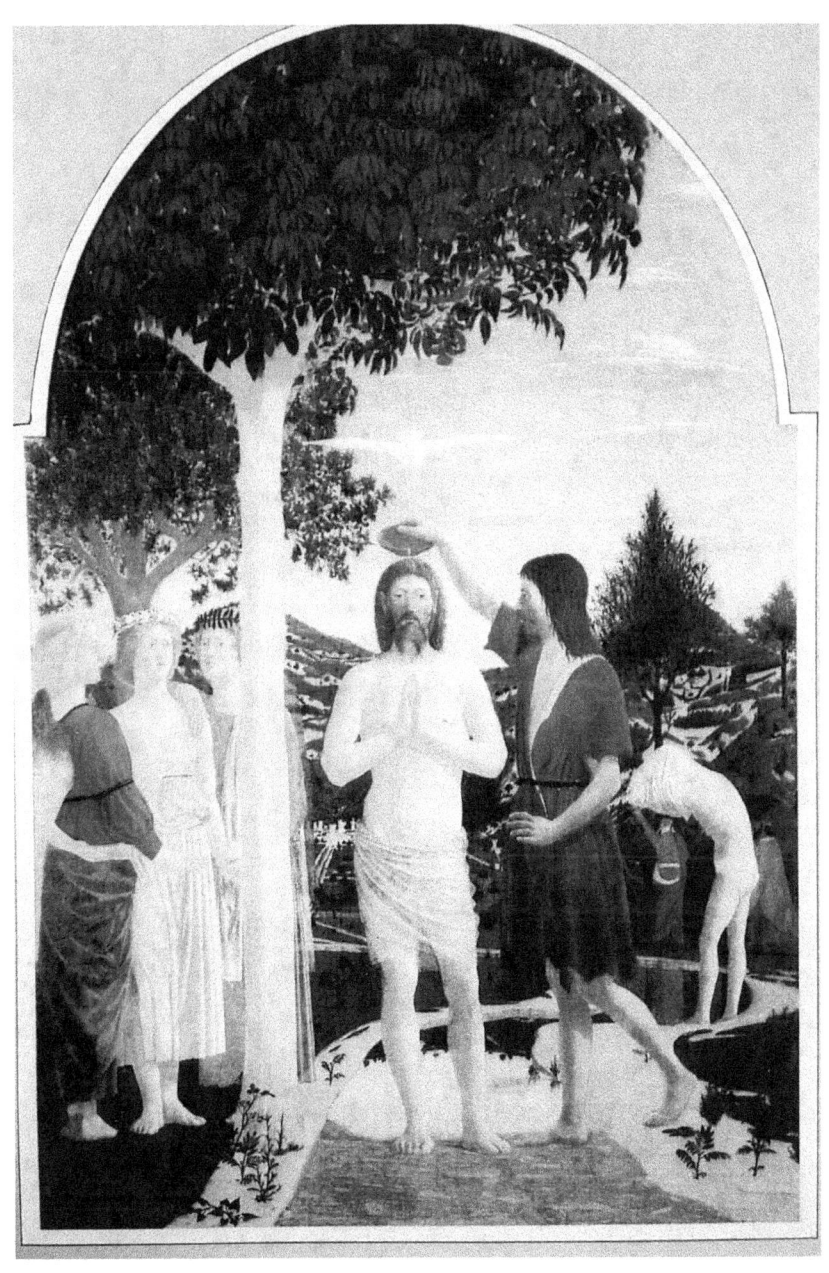

Piero della Francesca, *The Baptism of Christ*, National Gallery, London

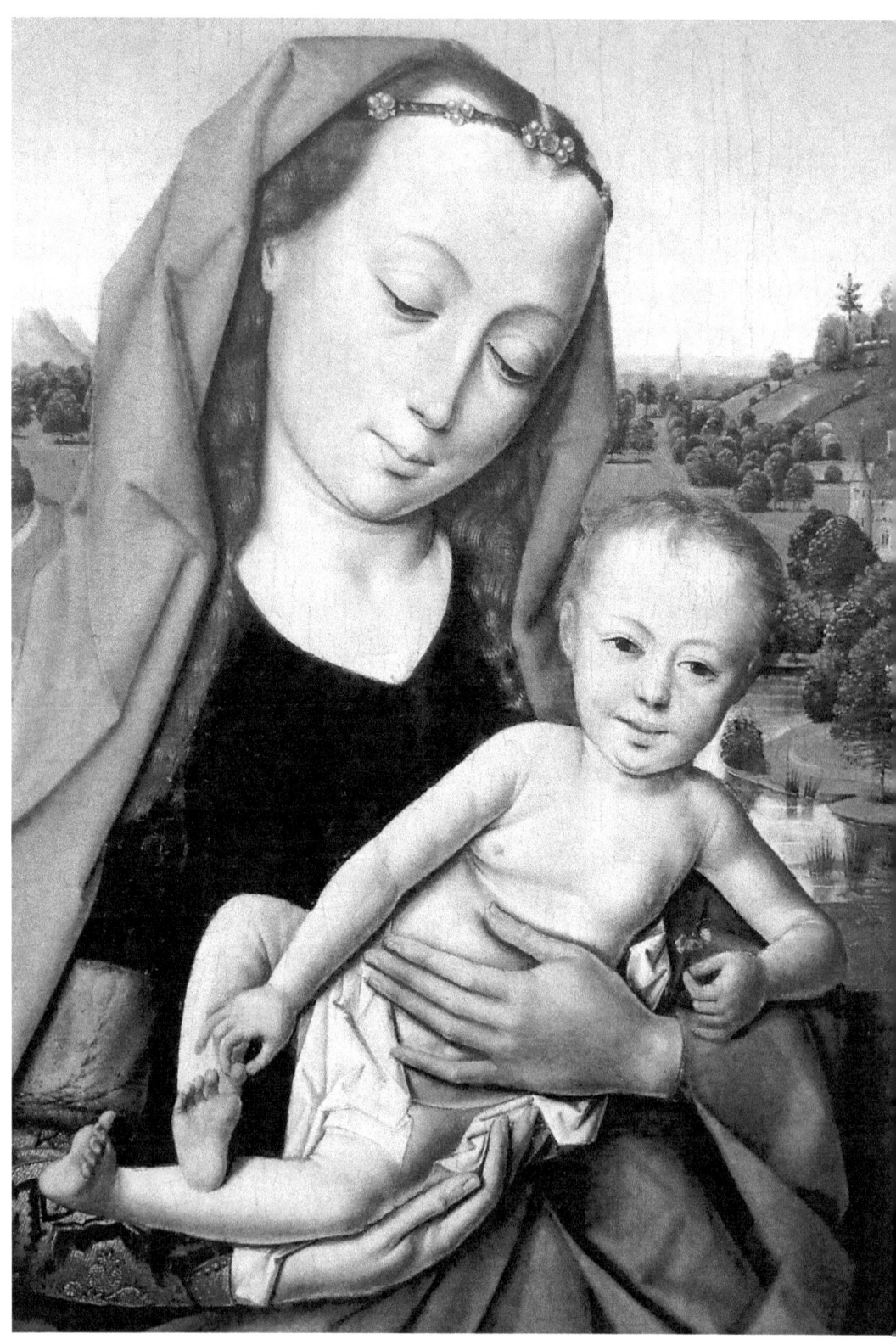

Dieric Bouts (workshop), Virgin and Child, Metropolitan Museum, New York City

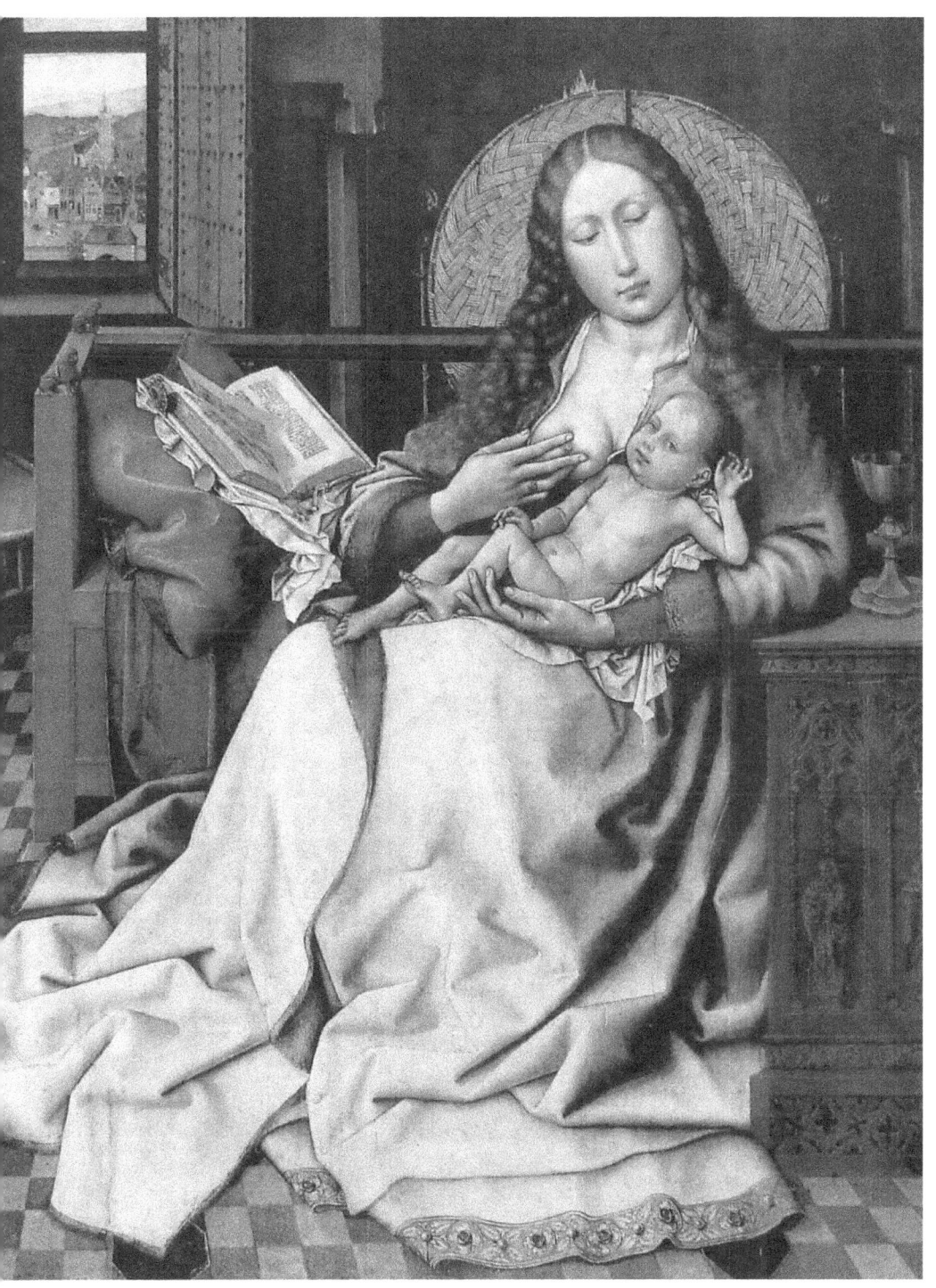

Robert Campin, Madonna With the Firescreen, National Gallery, London

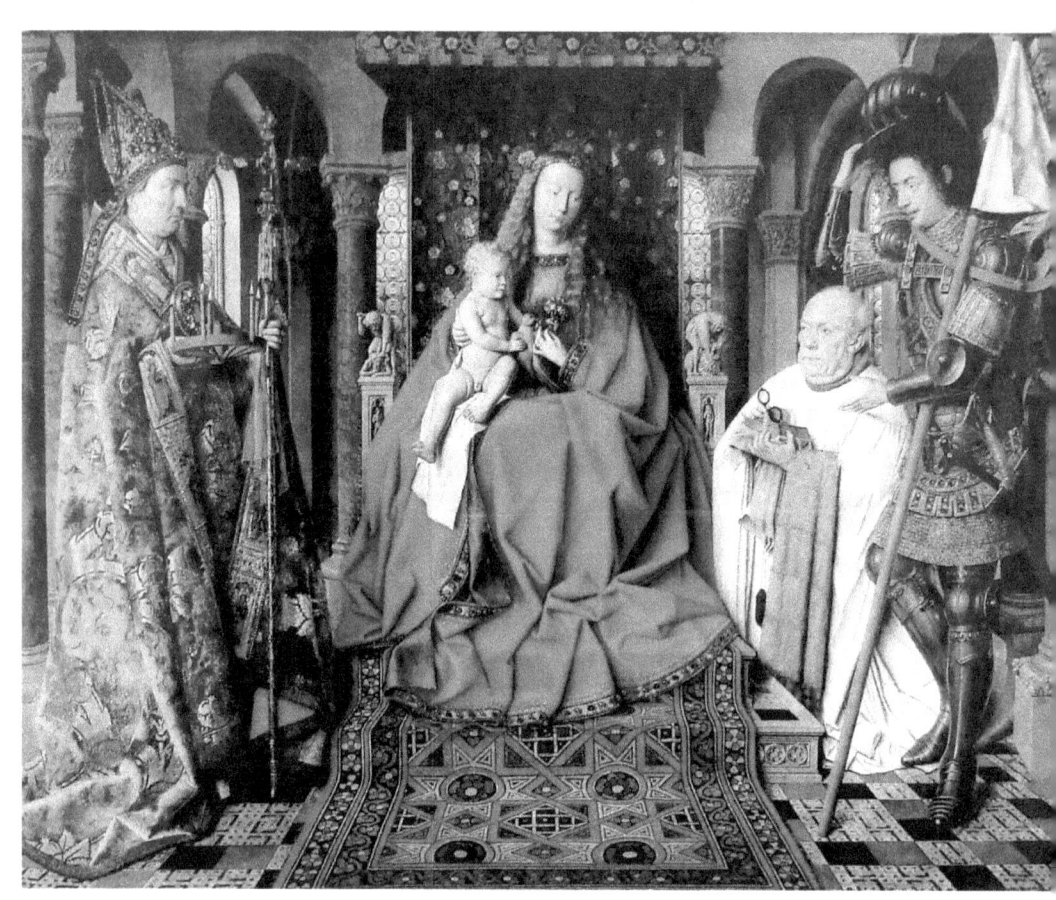

Jan van Eyck, The Paele Madonna, 1436, Bruges

GIOTTO BIBLIOGRAPHY

A LIST OF THE PRINCIPAL BOOKS AND MAGAZINE
ARTICLES DEALING WITH GIOTTO

Alexandre, A. Histoire populaire de la peinture: école
italienne. (Paris, 1894) – Baldinucci, F. Notizie dei professori del
disegno da Cimabue in quà. (Florence, 1681) – Berenson, B.
Florentine Painters of the Renaissance. (New York, 1896) –
Blashfield, E. H. and E. W. Italian Cities. (New York, 1900) –
Breton, E. Ambrogio Bondone dit le Giotto. (St. Germain-en-Laye,
1851) – Burckhardt, J. Der Cicerone, edited by W. Bode. (Leipsic,
1898) – Callcott, Lady. Description of the Chapel of the
Annunziata dell' Arena in Padua. (London, 1835) – Cartwright, J.
The Painters of Florence. (London, 1901) – Cennini, C. Treatise on
Painting: Trans. by Mrs. Merrifield. (London, 1844) – Colvin, S.
'Giotto' in 'Encyclopædia Britannica.' (Edinburgh, 1883) – Crowe,
J. A., and Cavalcaselle, G. B. History of Painting in Italy.
(London, 1866) – Dobbert, E. 'Giotto' in 'Dohme's Kunst und
Künstler,' etc. (Leipsic, 1878) – Fea, C. Descrizione della cappella
di S. Francesco d'Assisi. (Rome, 1820) – Förster, E. Beiträge zur
neuern Kunstgeschichte. (Leipsic, 1835) – Frantz, E. Geschichte
der christlichen Malerei. (Freiburg im Breisgau, 1887-94) –
Ghiberti, L. Commentario sulle arti. (Extracts from manuscript
copy are quoted by Milanesi, Cicognara, Perkins, and Frey) –

Gordon, L. D. The Story of Assisi. (London, 1900) – Hoppin, J. M. Great Epochs in Art History. (Boston, 1901) – Jameson, A. Memoirs of Italian Painters. (Boston, 1896) – Janitschek, H. Die Kunstlehre Dante's und Giotto's Kunst. (Leipsic, 1892) – Kugler, F. T. Italian Schools of Painting. Revised by A. H. Layard. (London, 1900) – Kuhn, P. A. Allgemeine Kunst-Geschichte. (Einsiedeln, 1891 et seq.) – Lee, V. Euphorion. (London, 1884) – Lindsay, Lord. Sketches of the History of Christian Art. (London, 1885) – Lübke, W. History of Art. (New York, 1878) – Mantz, P. Chefs-d'œuvre de la peinture italienne. (Paris, 1870) – Müntz, E. Histoire de l' Art pendant la Renaissance: Les Primitifs. (Paris, 1889) – Oliphant, Mrs. The Makers of Florence. (London, 1888) – Perkins, F. M. Giotto. (London, 1901) – Quilter, H. Giotto. (London, 1880) – Rio, A. F. De l' Art chrétien. (Paris, 1861-7) – Rumohr, C. F. v. Italienische Forschungen. (Berlin, 1827) – Ruskin, J. Giotto and his Works in Padua. (London, 1854) – Ruskin, J. Fors Clavigera. (Orpington, 1883) – Ruskin, J. Mornings in Florence. (Orpington, 1875) – Ruskin, J. Modern Painters. (London, 1846-60) – Sacchetti, F. Delle Novelle. (Florence, 1724) – Schnaase, C. Geschichte der bildenden Künste. (Düsseldorf, 1843-4) – Selvatico, P. E. Sulla cappellina degli Scrovegni nell' Arena di Padova. (Padua, 1836) – Stillman, W. J. Old Italian Masters. (New York, 1892) – Symonds, J. A. Renaissance in Italy. (London, 1875) – Taine, H. Voyage en Italie. (Paris, 1866) – Thode, H. Franz von Assisi. (Berlin, 1885) – Thode, H. Giotto. (Leipsic, 1899) – Tikkanen, J. J. Der Malerische Styl Giotto's. (Helsingfors, 1884) – Vasari, G. Lives of the Painters. (New York, 1897) – Woltmann, A., and Woermann, K. History of Painting: Trans. by Clara Bell. (New York, 1895) – Zimmermann, M. G. Giotto und die Kunst Italiens in Mittelalter. (Leipsic, 1899).

MAGAZINE ARTICLES

Archivio storico dell'arte, 1892: 'Die Kunstlehre Dante's und Giotto's Kunst' di Janitschek (C. de Fabriczy) – Century Magazine, 1889: Giotto (W. J. Stillman) – Jahrbuch der Preussischen Kunstsammlungen, 1885 and 1886: Studien zu Giotto (K. Frey) – Monthly Review, 1900: Art before Giotto (R. E. Fry). 1900: Giotto (R. E. Fry). 1901: Giotto (R. E. Fry) – Nuova Antologia, 1867: Giotto (C. Laderchi). 1875: Aneddoto dell' O e la supposta gita di Giotto ad Avignone (G. B. Cavalcaselle). 1880: La chiesa di Giotto nell' Arena di Padova (C. Boito). 1881: San Francesco, Dante e Giotto (G. Mestica). 1900: Dante e Giotto (A. Venturi) – Penn Monthly, 1881: Cimabue and Giotto (W. de B. Fryer) – Portfolio, 1882: Assisi (J. Cartwright) – Repertorium für Kunstwissenschaft, 1897: Die Heimath Giotto's (R. Davidsohn). 1899: Die Fresken im Querschiff der Unterkirche San Francesco (P. Schubring) – Revue de l'Art chrétien, 1873: Evolutions de l'Art chrétien (G. d. Saint-Laurent). 1885: Giotto. Naturalisme et mysticisme (E. Cartier). 1885: Le Poème de Giotto. (E. Cartier) – Zeitschrift für bildende Kunst, 1898 and 1899: Die malerische Dekoration der S. Francesco-kirche in Assisi (A. Aubert).

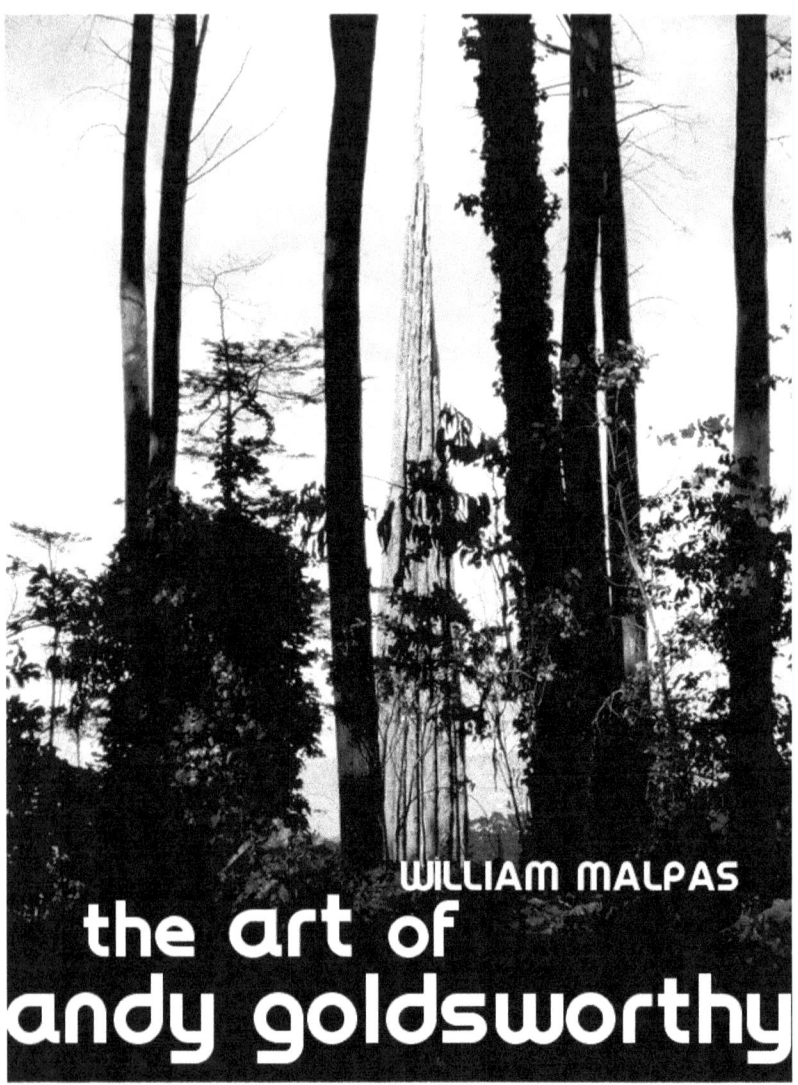

WILLIAM MALPAS

the art of
andy goldsworthy

This is the most comprehensive and detailed account of the art of Andy Goldsworthy available.

This study of Andy Goldsworthy discusses all of Goldsworthy's major exhibitions, books and projects, including the *Sheepfolds* project; *Garden of Stones* in New York; TV and dance collaborations; and the books *Wood, Stone, Time* and *Passage*. William Malpas surveys all of Goldsworthy's output, and analyzes his relation with other land artists such as Robert Smithson, the Christos, Walter de Maria, Chris Drury, Richard Long and David Nash; women sculptors; sculpture in the modern era; and Goldsworthy's place in the contemporary British art scene.

The book has been updated and revised for this new edition.

ISBN 9781861714107 Pbk   ISBN 9781861714114 Hbk
Fully illustrated   www.crmoon.com

MAURICE SENDAK

& the art of children's book illustration

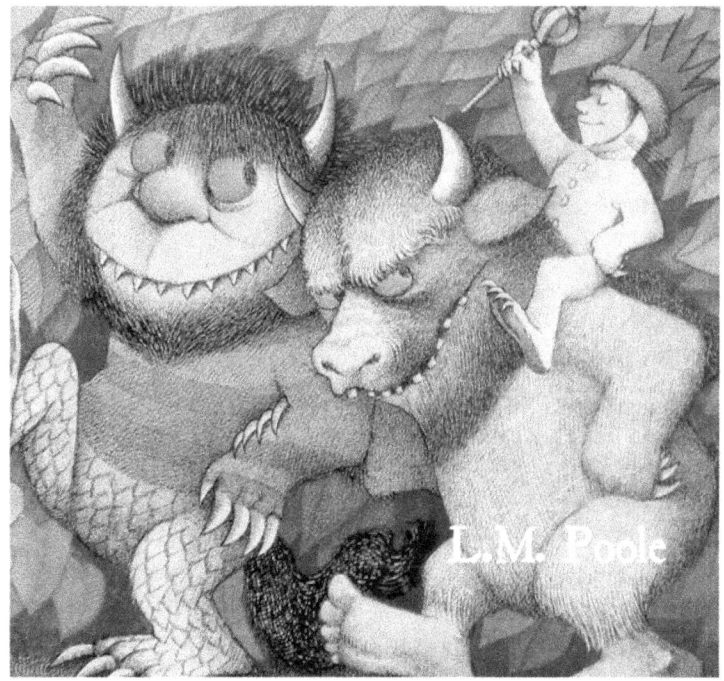

Maurice Sendak is the widely acclaimed American children's book author and illustrator. This critical study focuses on his famous trilogy, *Where the Wild Things Are, In the Night Kitchen* and *Outside Over There,* as well as the early works and Sendak's superb depictions of the Grimm Brothers' fairy tales in *The Juniper Tree.* L.M. Poole begins with a chapter on children's book illustration, in particular the treatment of fairy tales. Sendak's work is situated within the history of children's book illustration, and he is compared with many contemporary authors.

Fully illustrated. The book has been revised and updated for this edition.
ISBN 9781861714282 Pbk   ISBN 9781861713469 Hbk

CRESCENT MOON PUBLISHING

web: www.crmoon.com e-mail: cresmopub@yahoo.co.uk

ARTS, PAINTING, SCULPTURE

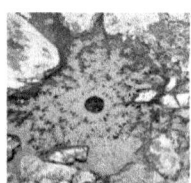

The Art of Andy Goldsworthy
Andy Goldsworthy: Touching Nature
Andy Goldsworthy in Close-Up
Andy Goldsworthy: Pocket Guide
Andy Goldsworthy In America

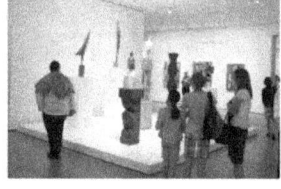

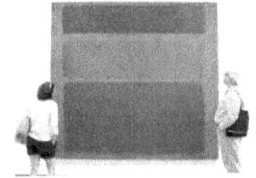

Land Art: A Complete Guide
The Art of Richard Long
Richard Long: Pocket Guide
Land Art In the UK
Land Art in Close-Up
Land Art In the U.S.A.
Land Art: Pocket Guide
Installation Art in Close-Up
Minimal Art and Artists In the 1960s and After
Colourfield Painting
Land Art DVD, TV documentary
Andy Goldsworthy DVD, TV documentary
The Erotic Object: Sexuality in Sculpture From Prehistory to the Present Day
Sex in Art: Pornography and Pleasure in Painting and Sculpture
Postwar Art
Sacred Gardens: The Garden in Myth, Religion and Art
Glorification: Religious Abstraction in Renaissance and 20th Century Art
Early Netherlandish Painting
Leonardo da Vinci
Piero della Francesca
Giovanni Bellini

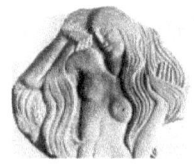

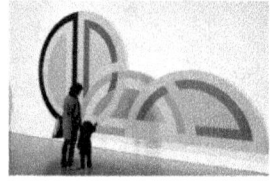

Fra Angelico: Art and Religion in the Renaissance
Mark Rothko: The Art of Transcendence
Frank Stella: American Abstract Artist
Jasper Johns
Brice Marden

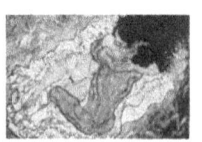

Alison Wilding: The Embrace of Sculpture
Vincent van Gogh: Visionary Landscapes
Eric Gill: Nuptials of God
Constantin Brancusi: Sculpting the Essence of Things

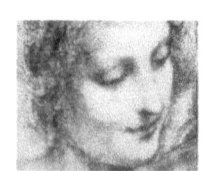

Max Beckmann
Caravaggio
Gustave Moreau
Egon Schiele: Sex and Death In Purple Stockings
Delizioso Fotografico Fervore: Works In Process 1
Sacro Cuore: Works In Process 2
The Light Eternal: J.M.W. Turner
The Madonna Glorified: Karen Arthurs

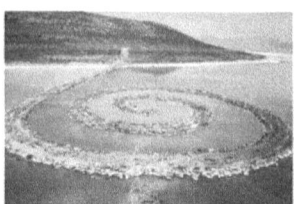

LITERATURE

J.R.R. Tolkien: The Books, The Films, The Whole Cultural Phenomenon
J.R.R. Tolkien: Pocket Guide
Tolkien's Heroic Quest
The *Earthsea* Books of Ursula Le Guin
Beauties, Beasts and Enchantment: Classic French Fairy Tales
German Popular Stories by the Brothers Grimm
Philip Pullman and *His Dark Materials*
Sexing Hardy: Thomas Hardy and Feminism
Thomas Hardy's *Tess of the d'Urbervilles*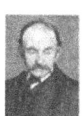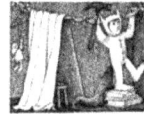
Thomas Hardy's *Jude the Obscure*
Thomas Hardy: The Tragic Novels
Love and Tragedy: Thomas Hardy
The Poetry of Landscape in Hardy
Wessex Revisited: Thomas Hardy and John Cowper Powys
Wolfgang Iser: Essays and Interviews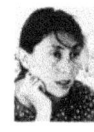
Petrarch, Dante and the Troubadours
Maurice Sendak and the Art of Children's Book Illustration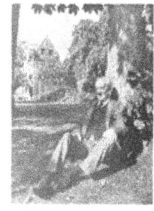
Andrea Dworkin
Cixous, Irigaray, Kristeva: The *Jouissance* of French Feminism
Julia Kristeva: Art, Love, Melancholy, Philosophy, Semiotics and Psychoanalysis
Hélène Cixous I Love You: The *Jouissance* of Writing
Luce Irigaray: Lips, Kissing, and the Politics of Sexual Difference
Peter Redgrove: Here Comes the Flood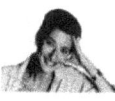
Peter Redgrove: Sex-Magic-Poetry-Cornwall
Lawrence Durrell: Between Love and Death, East and West
Love, Culture & Poetry: Lawrence Durrell
Cavafy: Anatomy of a Soul
German Romantic Poetry: Goethe, Novalis, Heine, Hölderlin
Feminism and Shakespeare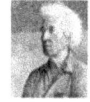
Shakespeare: Love, Poetry & Magic
The Passion of D.H. Lawrence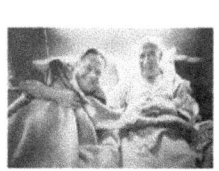
D.H. Lawrence: Symbolic Landscapes
D.H. Lawrence: Infinite Sensual Violence
Rimbaud: Arthur Rimbaud and the Magic of Poetry
The Ecstasies of John Cowper Powys
Sensualism and Mythology: The Wessex Novels of John Cowper Powys
Amorous Life: John Cowper Powys and the Manifestation of Affectivity (H.W. Fawkner)
Postmodern Powys: New Essays on John Cowper Powys (Joe Boulter)
Rethinking Powys: Critical Essays on John Cowper Powys
Paul Bowles & Bernardo Bertolucci
Rainer Maria Rilke
Joseph Conrad: *Heart of Darkness*
In the Dim Void: Samuel Beckett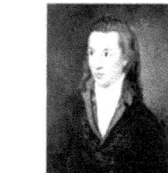
Samuel Beckett Goes into the Silence
André Gide: Fiction and Fervour
Jackie Collins and the Blockbuster Novel
Blinded By Her Light: The Love-Poetry of Robert Graves
The Passion of Colours: Travels In Mediterranean Lands
Poetic Forms

POETRY

Ursula Le Guin: Walking In Cornwall
Peter Redgrove: Here Comes The Flood
Peter Redgrove: Sex-Magic-Poetry-Cornwall
Dante: Selections From the Vita Nuova
Petrarch, Dante and the Troubadours
William Shakespeare: Sonnets
William Shakespeare: Complete Poems
Blinded By Her Light: The Love-Poetry of Robert Graves
Emily Dickinson: Selected Poems
Emily Brontë: Poems
Thomas Hardy: Selected Poems
Percy Bysshe Shelley: Poems
John Keats: Selected Poems
Joh n Keats: Poems of 1820
D.H. Lawrence: Selected Poems
Edmund Spenser: Poems
Edmund Spenser: Amoretti
John Donne: Poems
Henry Vaughan: Poems
Sir Thomas Wyatt: Poems
Robert Herrick: Selected Poems
Rilke: Space, Essence and Angels in the Poetry of Rainer Maria Rilke
Rainer Maria Rilke: Selected Poems
Friedrich Hölderlin: Selected Poems
Arseny Tarkovsky: Selected Poems
Arthur Rimbaud: Selected Poems
Arthur Rimbaud: A Season in Hell
Arthur Rimbaud and the Magic of Poetry
Novalis: Hymns To the Night
German Romantic Poetry
Paul Verlaine: Selected Poems
Elizaethan Sonnet Cycles
D.J. Enright: By-Blows
Jeremy Reed: Brigitte's Blue Heart
Jeremy Reed: Claudia Schiffer's Red Shoes
Gorgeous Little Orpheus
Radiance: New Poems
Crescent Moon Book of Nature Poetry
Crescent Moon Book of Love Poetry
Crescent Moon Book of Mystical Poetry
Crescent Moon Book of Elizabethan Love Poetry
Crescent Moon Book of Metaphysical Poetry
Crescent Moon Book of Romantic Poetry
Pagan America: New American Poetry

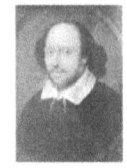
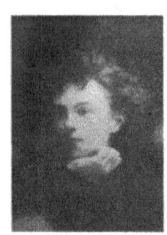
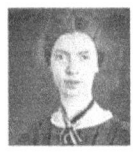
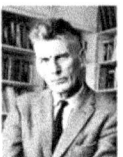
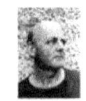
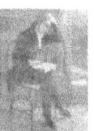
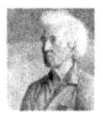
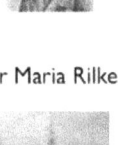
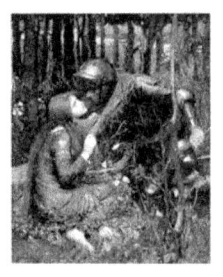
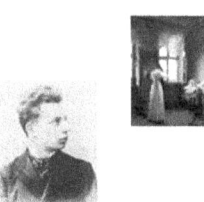
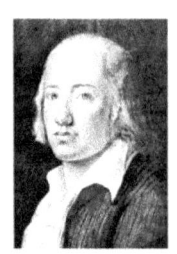
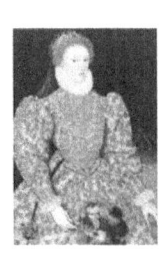

MEDIA, CINEMA, FEMINISM and CULTURAL STUDIES

J.R.R. Tolkien: The Books, The Films, The Whole Cultural Phenomenon
J.R.R. Tolkien: Pocket Guide
The *Lord of the Rings* Movies: Pocket Guide
The Cinema of Hayao Miyazaki
Hayao Miyazaki: *Princess Mononoke*: Pocket Movie Guide
Hayao Miyazaki: *Spirited Away*: Pocket Movie Guide
Tim Burton : Hallowe'en For Hollywood
Ken Russell
Ken Russell: *Tommy*: Pocket Movie Guide
The Ghost Dance: The Origins of Religion
The Peyote Cult
Cixous, Irigaray, Kristeva: The *Jouissance* of French Feminism
Julia Kristeva: Art, Love, Melancholy, Philosophy, Semiotics and Psychoanalysis
Luce Irigaray: Lips, Kissing, and the Politics of Sexual Difference
Hélene Cixous I Love You: The *Jouissance* of Writing
Andrea Dworkin
'Cosmo Woman': The World of Women's Magazines
Women in Pop Music
HomeGround: The Kate Bush Anthology
Discovering the Goddess (Geoffrey Ashe)
The Poetry of Cinema
The Sacred Cinema of Andrei Tarkovsky
Andrei Tarkovsky: Pocket Guide
Andrei Tarkovsky: *Mirror*: Pocket Movie Guide
Andrei Tarkovsky: *The Sacrifice*: Pocket Movie Guide
Walerian Borowczyk: Cinema of Erotic Dreams
Jean-Luc Godard: The Passion of Cinema
Jean-Luc Godard: *Hail Mary*: Pocket Movie Guide
Jean-Luc Godard: *Contempt*: Pocket Movie Guide
Jean-Luc Godard: *Pierrot le Fou*: Pocket Movie Guide
John Hughes and Eighties Cinema
Ferris Bueller's Day Off: Pocket Movie Guide
Jean-Luc Godard: Pocket Guide
The Cinema of Richard Linklater
Liv Tyler: Star In Ascendance
Blade Runner and the Films of Philip K. Dick
Paul Bowles and Bernardo Bertolucci
Media Hell: Radio, TV and the Press
An Open Letter to the BBC
Detonation Britain: Nuclear War in the UK
Feminism and Shakespeare
Wild Zones: Pornography, Art and Feminism
Sex in Art: Pornography and Pleasure in Painting and Sculpture
Sexing Hardy: Thomas Hardy and Feminism

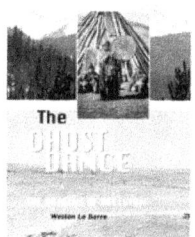
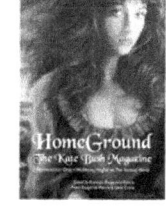
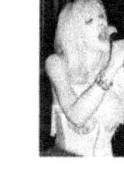
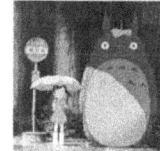
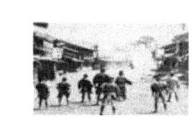
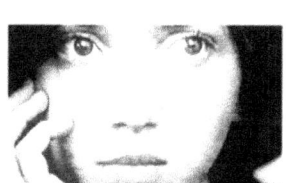

The Light Eternal is a model monograph, an exemplary job. The subject matter of the book is beautifully
organised and dead on beam. (Lawrence Durrell)
It is amazing for me to see my work treated with such passion and respect. (Andrea Dworkin)

CRESCENT MOON PUBLISHING
P.O. Box 1312, Maidstone, Kent, ME14 5XU, Great Britain. www.crmoon.com

cresmopub@yahoo.co.uk   www.crescentmoon.org.uk

www.ingramcontent.com/pod-product-compliance
Lightning Source LLC
Chambersburg PA
CBHW051326220526
45468CB00004B/1521